ANDREW JENNINGS
SENTENCE
NINJA

BLOOMSBURY EDUCATION

LONDON OXFORD NEW YORK NEW DELHI SYDNEY

BLOOMSBURY EDUCATION
Bloomsbury Publishing Plc
50 Bedford Square, London, WC1B 3DP, UK
29 Earlsfort Terrace, Dublin 2, Ireland

BLOOMSBURY, BLOOMSBURY EDUCATION and the Diana logo are trademarks of Bloomsbury Publishing Plc

First published in Great Britain, 2025 by Bloomsbury Publishing Plc

This edition published in Great Britain, 2025 by Bloomsbury Publishing Plc

Text copyright © Andrew Jennings, 2025

Andrew Jennings has asserted his right under the Copyright, Designs and Patents Act, 1988, to be identified as Author of this work

Bloomsbury Publishing Plc does not have any control over, or responsibility for, any third-party websites referred to or in this book. All internet addresses given in this book were correct at the time of going to press. The author and publisher regret any inconvenience caused if addresses have changed or sites have ceased to exist, but can accept no responsibility for any such changes

All rights reserved. This book may be photocopied, for use in the educational establishment for which it was purchased, but may not be reproduced in any other form or by any other means – graphic, electronic, or mechanical, including photocopying, recording, taping or information storage or retrieval systems – without prior permission in writing of the publishers

A catalogue record for this book is available from the British Library

ISBN: PB: 978-1-8019-9566-5; ePDF: 978-1-8019-9567-2

2 4 6 8 10 9 7 5 3 1 (paperback)

Text design by Marcus Duck

Printed and bound in India by Manipal Technologies Limited.

To find out more about our authors and books visit www.bloomsbury.com and sign up for our newsletters

This book is dedicated to all the fabulous pupils I have taught throughout my career. Thank you for always inspiring me to think more deeply about how best to help you become confident and skilled writers.

OTHER NINJA RESOURCES FOR TEACHERS

COMPREHENSION NINJA NON-FICTION

A set of six books for ages 5–11 that provide carefully curated resources to teach the key reading comprehension skills. With strong links to the National Curriculum, each book presents 24 high-quality non-fiction texts and photocopiable activities that help embed reading skills and improve comprehension, using strategies and question types such as true or false, labelling, matching, highlighting, filling in the gap, sequencing and multiple choice.

COMPREHENSION NINJA FICTION AND POETRY

Each book in this six-book set contains 24 immersive fiction extracts and poetry texts by acclaimed writers including Roald Dahl, Michael Morpurgo, Patrice Lawrence, Katherine Rundell, David Almond, Zanib Mian, Joseph Coelho and Polly Ho-Yen. Every text is accompanied by photocopiable comprehension activities to boost reading retrieval skills in Key Stages 1 and 2.

NINJA MATHS RESOURCES

TIMES TABLES NINJA
SARAH FARRELL WITH ANDREW JENNINGS

The activities in these photocopiable books give Key Stage 1 and Key Stage 2 pupils all the tools they need to gain fluency in multiplication and division. The KS1 book focuses on the 2, 3, 4, 5 and 10 times tables, while the KS2 book covers the 2 to 12 times tables in detail, ready for the Year 4 multiplication tables check.

ARITHMETIC NINJA
ANDREW JENNINGS WITH SARAH FARRELL AND PAUL TUCKER

The Arithmetic Ninja series is the perfect resource for any primary classroom. Ideal for daily maths practice and quick lesson starters, each photocopiable book includes 10 questions per day and 39 bonus weekly ninja challenges – 702 question cards in total.

FOR CHILDREN AT HOME AND IN THE CLASSROOM

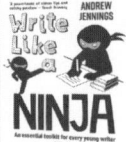

WRITE LIKE A NINJA

A pocket-sized book packed full of all the grammar, vocabulary and sentence structures that children need in order to improve and develop their writing skills. Fully aligned to the Key Stage 2 National Curriculum, this book is designed to be used independently by pupils.

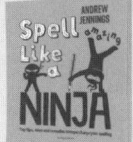

SPELL LIKE A NINJA

This book provides essential tips, lists and advice to support the teaching and learning of spelling in the classroom or at home. Including every statutory spelling pattern in the National Curriculum, this all-in-one quick reference tool enables pupils to learn at their own pace.

FURTHER RESOURCES FOR SCHOOLS, TEACHERS AND CHILDREN ONLINE

Head to www.vocabularyninja.co.uk and follow @VocabularyNinja on X (formerly Twitter) for more teaching and learning resources to support the teaching of vocabulary, reading, writing and the wider primary curriculum.

CONTENTS

PART 1 – THE WAY OF THE SENTENCE NINJA

Introduction	9
Sentence-level progression	14
Understanding the Sentence Ninja progression	21

PART 2 – GRAND MASTER SUBJECT KNOWLEDGE

Essential subject knowledge	26
Photocopiable activities – subject and verb	28

PART 3 – SENTENCE NINJA TOOLKIT: SENTENCE SUBJECT KNOWLEDGE

Essential subject knowledge	36
Compound sentences	38
Coordinating conjunctions – meanings and function	40
Complex sentences	45
Subordinating conjunctions – meanings and function	48
Relative clauses	55

PART 4 – ESSENTIAL SENTENCE NINJA TOOLKIT: PRACTICE

Simple sentences (subject + verb)	60
Compound sentences (coordinating conjunction)	64
Complex sentences (subordinating conjunction)	76
Relative clauses (relative pronoun)	88
Relative embedded clauses	97
PACE milestones	106
Create and connect	126
Make the reader feel	129
Build and vary	131
Answers	138

PART 1
THE WAY OF THE SENTENCE NINJA

INTRODUCTION

WELCOME

Hello and welcome to *Sentence Ninja*! It's fabulous to have you with us on this journey of sentence-level awakening and enlightenment. *Sentence Ninja* is your complete toolkit to improving pupils' ability to create well-structured sentences independently. Simple! Yup, and that's what this book aims to do … keep it simple, cut through the policies and progressions and provide clarity on how to improve sentences in your classrooms and schools.

Sentence Ninja aims to provide a clear guide to sentence-level improvement across the whole school. This includes subject knowledge, sentence progressions, teachable sentence toolkits and outstanding photocopiable resources to enable regular practice in school.

School Focus: Start to implement a consistent and universally agreed progression of sentence types across the school.

Teacher Focus: Equip teachers with the subject knowledge and resources to prepare, teach, track and assess sentence-level competence of their pupils.

Pupil Focus: Build sentence-level confidence as well as a secure toolkit of sentence types that pupils can apply easily within their any writing.

Well you're here, so I'm guessing there's a problem. So let's talk about sentences and teaching. But first, let's get REAL! Real about everything that surrounds the teaching of any aspect of the curriculum well. We need to deal in the realities and realisms of the situation. It helps that I'm speaking from over a decade of my own experience as a teacher and leader in many different KS1, KS2 and even KS3 settings, trying to combat what feels like a plague of sentence-level insecurity. But how can it be that pupils arriving in KS3 aged 11 and 12, having been in hour-long literacy lessons on pretty much a daily basis for the past six or seven years, can't write a few correctly structured sentences? Now, don't get me wrong, this isn't all pupils, absolutely not! But, despite the best efforts of so many hard-working and dedicated teachers, huge numbers of pupils still can't develop basic sentence- level structures independently.

Sentences are arguably one of the single most important 'things' our children will be taught in school, but sentences are quite often a subject of great misunderstanding and genuine lack of confidence for so many of our pupils.

I dare you to ask the next pupil you encounter in school, 'What is a sentence?'. For most pupils, and potentially many teachers (myself once included here), they might just be wishing for the ground to open and swallow them whole. OK, that's all a little dramatic, but I'd pretty much guarantee that you would get answers that were incredibly unsure or that were wildly inconsistent.

Either way, the phrases 'incredibly unsure' and 'wildly inconsistent' are not really what we want to be associating with high-quality teaching and learning. We would really like to see the opposite of those two phrases to be true. Every child and adult in our schools should easily and confidently be able to respond to this question, and we'll uncover how simple the answer is soon enough.

So, why are sentences so misunderstood? There are potentially many factors that contribute to the downfall of sentences in our schools.

Training: Teacher training, from memory, is an intense process that has to cover so much ground in what is such a short space of time. This can mean that, even though subject knowledge is included in the training, it can often take a back seat.

Time: We need time to teach sentences, time to practise, time to dig a little deeper and understand sentences more. Although time in teaching is so often against us, hopefully this book will provide solutions to this problem.

CPD/whole-school vision: If sentences really are to be taught well, they need to be prioritised from the top down, where the curriculum allows for sentence-level teaching and practice within an English or literacy lesson.

Assumption: Is it the assumption that sentence-level teaching is prioritised or taught well, when this isn't necessarily the case? Ultimately, we may have pupils higher up the school who aren't capable of confidently constructing varied sentences.

Lack of dedicated discrete teaching: The demands of the curriculum, or to generate writing outcomes, can often be at the detriment of focusing on what really matters … the sentence.

Practice: Practice is often misinterpreted as copying and as a result is not encouraged. We need to look at how practice is perceived and, more importantly, valued if we are to see the positive changes we desire.

Now this isn't all about painting a negative picture about sentences and teaching. There's a huge amount of outstanding teaching of sentences and writing to be seen. But there are also many teachers who find themselves, due to the reasons above, in a position where sentence-level standards in their classrooms, year on year, just aren't improving – despite everyone's effort.

First we need a reality check! We need to look at the reality of writing in our school and understand what is *going to* make a real difference versus what we *think will* make a difference.

REALITY CHECK

This is a great point to take a reality check and ask some questions about writing in your classroom or school. You may be a class teacher, subject leader, member of the SLT, or even have responsibility for all of these roles. So it's important to consider your role and the impact you can have. Try not to kid yourself too; be honest.

- Would everyone in your school (pupils and staff) be able to consistently explain what a sentence is?
- Do you and/or your staff regularly and explicitly teach different types of sentences?
- Do you and/or your staff dedicate time to practising how to write specific sentence types?
- Do you and/or your staff have a strong grammatical understanding of different sentences?
- Does your school have a consistent approach and terminology for teaching sentences?

If the answers to these questions are tending to edge towards 'no', then we need to start to understand and visualise the reality of the problem and how we can go about solving it.

ARE OUR PUPILS 'MATCH READY'?

Here's an analogy to help us visualise where we need to be with sentences, both in terms of our approach and the outcomes we want to achieve. There are so many real-life examples of how practice is the key ingredient to success in nearly every aspect of learning and life, and yet in education this often goes out of the window.

Let's use football as a common ground. Even at a grassroots level of any sport, a coach will emphasise to children the importance of practising regularly. Yes, playing matches is important, but during a match you might only touch the ball seven or eight times, so we are unlikely to improve technically by playing a match (the outcome), or just by doing more matches (writing outcomes). The only way to really improve technically is to practise, under the instruction of a coach (the teacher who has experience) when needed for specific instruction, and then solo practise over and over again until we develop an independent level of competence or skill. Then we can apply it in the match (or writing outcome). Makes sense, doesn't it? And yet, in so many settings, I've seen just more and more matches being played.

Even the most famous and successful sports people – for example, Cristiano Ronaldo, Kobe Bryant or Dame Kelly Holmes – cite their dedication to practice as being key to their success, despite being naturally gifted at their chosen sport. Practice and training are the things that make them great. And let's remember, not all of our pupils are naturally gifted at writing, so practice for them is even more crucial. Imagine asking a child who has never really kicked a football before to go and play for the school team in a competitive game. It wouldn't be a nice experience for the child. If we then ask that child to play more matches, they will become acclimatised to the traumatic environment we keep putting them in, but they won't be successful and they won't improve technically. We have to realise the reality of asking children to just keep writing more often.

If practice is the key ingredient to success in the development of nearly every skill, why do we not ask children to practise how to write sentences? And why don't we encourage them to practise writing sentences to a point where they are awesome at crafting a wide range of different sentences? Well fortunately, that's what this book is all about. *Sentence Ninja* is going to keep it super simple and take you from the basics of what a sentence is, to providing an effective teachable toolkit that can be applied across your whole school.

ARE OUR WRITERS EQUIPPED FOR SUCCESS? DO WE HAVE A STRATEGY?

Essentially, a writing outcome is a problem to be solved; a challenge, an opportunity to express ourself as a person. We need to come up with a solution.

In maths, we teach a range of strategies to equip pupils to be able to successfully answer a given problem. Adding fractions, long division or calculating area all require an element of subject knowledge that is then applied via a strategy or a skill, which has been practised regularly to build confidence. However, testing pupils more frequently doesn't make them any more successful at tests. Linking back to writing, this continues to ring true as the writing outcome is essentially a test of our ability to write.

The reality of writing, once again, is overcomplicated. After children leave school, 99.9 per cent of them will never need to write fairy tales, recounts of trips, newspaper reports or diary entries. More importantly, our primary pupils need to be able to articulate their thoughts and ideas clearly and with variation, ready for GCSE and life beyond school. We can build those foundations right now. We need to simplify our vision of what is valuable: the ability to create grammatically sound sentences independently, with some level of variation.

When pupils are equipped with multiple strategies and knowledge, they can apply these skills and strategies independently and problem-solve, ultimately becoming more successful with the test environment. As teachers, we must actively think about what this 'sentence-level toolkit' looks like for writing and how it is going to equip all our pupils inclusively and effectively for the challenges of writing in our settings.

Being able to write clear, varied, and well-structured sentences is an essential skill that all children need to be able to do, and actually it's not that difficult. We just need to understand and prioritise the basics, have a clear progression and practise regularly, and be supported by explicit instruction.

PRACTICE – OUR HIDDEN SECRET WEAPON

As teachers, it's inbuilt in us to naturally assess and look for solutions to improve and develop our pupils, moving them on in their educational journey. So, it's especially infuriating when, despite our best efforts and all the high-quality teaching that our pupils receive, the basic skill of creating coherent sentences just seems to stagnate.

Well, here's the solution. **We need to learn to love the basics. To live and breathe them**. It can't always be about the superlatives, forced semicolon use and pathetic fallacy, which I have seen creep into so many lessons over the years. And yes, some children who are secure are possibly ready for this, but so many more aren't – not because they won't understand it or won't be able to do it, but because they can't do the basics. **We have to ensure that – wait, it's much more than that; it's our moral responsibility and pledge – our pupils have mastered the basics**. And let's spell it out: we have to ensure that they can write simple, compound and complex sentences without really having to think too much about it, because it's embedded. It's simple, and as teachers we need to take responsibility for this as a school, with everyone prioritising sentence-level teaching together – day after day, year after year!

Let's be honest, expected standard writing is basically just writing with sentences that are well structured and varied. If pupils can do that, then they are pretty much there. Yes, there are a few other grammatical features that need to be thrown in, but none of those are particularly tricky to teach or include. A good piece of expected standard writing at the end of KS2 will be made up of four to six paragraphs, most likely made up of five or six sentences each. So really, we need to train our pupils in the skill of creating those sentences, which create those paragraphs. A word of warning: we're not telling pupils that a paragraph is five to six sentences long or creating some type of archaic formula – we are instead creating a simple reality of what we need to equip and teach children to do.

WE NEED TO 'KEEP IT UP!' THE PROFOUND IMPACT OF PRACTICE

Here's a non-teaching real-life example that exemplifies the **principles of practice**!

My son (a football-mad nine-year-old in Year 5) attends Cubs. It's fab – if you have children, I'd highly recommend it. Recently, Akela (the pack leader) set the task of completing two personal challenges. My son loves football, so inevitably he decided that one of the challenges would be to do 40 keepy-uppies. If you don't know what a keepy-uppie is, it is basically kicking or 'keeping' the ball in the air without it hitting the floor, mostly with your feet. My son's challenge was to keep the ball up 40 times – his best at that time was about 10.

Let's unpick the whole situation from a teaching and learning perspective.

> **Outcome**: Child to complete 40 consecutive keepy-uppies.
>
> **Teacher (me)**: Highly skilled and experienced in the skill itself. Has shown the child many times how to perform the skill.
>
> **Assessment**: Child is currently capable of 10 keepy-uppies, maximum. He doesn't practise in a regular or focused fashion. He wants to be able to do it, but isn't really improving, despite playing football competitively for five years, including various regular training sessions.
>
> **Expectation: My expectation** is that my son **should** be able to perform this skill to a fairly high level already, but he can't.

In writing this, it hit me! It's really scary how similar this situation mimics how I felt about many pupils' writing abilities over the years, and **my expectations** of what they **should** have been able to do. Despite my skill level and my son's/my pupils' regular exposure, the outcome task (keepy-uppies/a piece of writing) and his/their skill level wasn't improving. It's interesting, isn't it?

This situation is extremely common, whereby a high-quality teacher/mentor with high personal knowledge and experience, teaches and models the skill to the pupil. So what's missing? The answer is **PRACTICE**! Regular, dedicated practice of the skill, with ongoing teaching throughout the journey.

When I trained to be a teacher, my wife and I bought a black Labrador puppy, Max. Sadly, he passed away recently. As a family, we made the decision to get a new yellow Labrador puppy, Merlin. In getting Merlin, I made a very conscious decision to commit to training him properly, by using expert advice (experienced teacher) and learning from past mistakes made with Max. So, as you do, I bought a book called *Easy Peasy Puppy Squeazy* by an expert dog trainer called Steve Mann. After trying to familiarise myself with the first few recommended basic and foundational skills of 'sit', 'down' and 'heel', the book moved on to discuss the importance of practice and 'taking skills on the road', which just means to practise the skills in different environments. Steve used this phrase: 'Don't trust the pup that has done a thousand exercises, trust the pup that has done one exercise a thousand times.' (Mann, 2019, p. 95)

What Steve is saying here is that within the plethora of skills and tricks I could teach Merlin – glossing over each one for a few days at a time and never really mastering any – the few that I will come to rely on are 'sit', 'down' and 'heel'. These are not only the absolute basics, but the basics that will be the foundations of keeping Merlin safe, making walks more enjoyable and making him an extremely reliable dog under any circumstance or environment. The same must be held true for our pupils' ability to construct sentences. To finish my puppy analogy, the mindset we need to adopt when it comes to teaching a puppy is exactly the mindset we need to adopt when teaching anything. Practice doesn't make perfect. Practice makes permanent.

As educators and leaders, we need to shift our mindsets and behold the serious value of dedicating time to practising.

CREATIVITY STEMS FROM CONFIDENCE IN SOLID FOUNDATIONS

As pupils move through school and continue to write, 'flair' and 'creativity' are the buzz words that ring loudly in teachers' ears, while often staring into writing books where pupils have produced half a page of writing without a full stop or a single conjunction. This is a sure-fire warning signal that the writing curriculum in a school is moving on far too quickly for pupils and that the basics of sentence structure are not embedded within the school. It isn't that the child hasn't understood what they have been taught; we just haven't equipped them with what they need, or given them the time to practise effectively to make these skills permanent.

For children to be able to demonstrate flair and creativity, we must first create young writers who have confidence in how to structure sentences one after another. Once they start to have this emerging confidence, children can show the flair that we really want to see, which is only enhanced further as it sits within well-structured and varied sentences.

SERIOUS ABOUT SENTENCES, PASSIONATE ABOUT PRACTICE

If a writing curriculum that is focused on writing outcomes just continues to move on, then there is no real way for pupils to genuinely catch up when it comes to their sentence-level ability. We provide checklists and opportunities to edit, but if the child doesn't independently know how to create different sentence structures at a grammatical level, then these sticky-plaster scaffolds won't help or make any real difference.

Despite the sentence-level writing doomsday rant, all is not lost. And, in actual fact, the solution itself is really simple, and this book is here to set you on the path to getting serious about sentences in your school and passionate about practice in your classrooms.

PROBLEMS, POLICIES AND PROGRESSIONS (AND DON'T FORGET PRACTICE)

Why do most writing policies and progressions all look pretty much the same?

A quick internet search for a 'primary writing policy' or a 'primary writing progression' will yield pretty much the same content, mapped out in a fairly similar fashion by schools across the country. Why is this? Well, everyone teaches from the same curriculum, so you'd expect the writing progressions to be very similar.

However, the other reason is, because schools are so busy, when a writing policy or progression is required, looking for examples where it's been done already, well, sort of makes sense. So we end up in a situation where lots of schools have progressions and policies that are replicated versions of another school's policy. The reason this is a problem is linked to the following question: why do most writing policies hardly mention sentences in any real detail?

If we can assume that all of the policies and progressions are derived from the primary National Curriculum, then this is the first problem that we encounter. We all know that the National Curriculum can be quite vague and, to a certain extent, requires quite a lot of the detail to be filled in by teachers and schools. With regards to the English part of the National Curriculum, Writing is broken down into 'transcription' and 'composition'. In KS1, sentences are covered with the phrases 'compose individual sentences' and 'combine to make sentences'. The whole of KS2 is covered with broad statements such as, 'use an increasing range of sentence structures'. That's it for composition on sentences. Following on from this, we are directed to the English Appendix 2 for Vocabulary, Grammar and Punctuation, where we get a little more detail on sentences.

If we look at the sentence row in each year group, we could argue that the bulk of the sentences we want our pupils to master – simple sentences (compound sentences using coordinating conjunctions) and complex sentences (using subordinating conjunctions) – are covered by the end of Year 2! And yet, lots of pupils in Year 5 and 6 still struggle to create these sentence structures.

In the National Curriculum, Year 3 focuses on developing phrases/clauses of time and place, Year 4 focuses mostly on the development of fronted adverbials, Year 5 looks at relative clauses, and Year 6 places emphasis on passive sentences. You could argue that all of these areas are relatively easy to teach and are actually more like grammatical tweaks and variations of a sentence.

I would argue that the sentence-level content is more critical in the success of writing for our pupils, and is the content we really need to 'make permanent'. According to the National Curriculum, this should have been mastered by the end of Year 2. I would personally suggest that, for many schools and teachers, this just isn't the writing reality within which we teach.

EVERY SENTENCE PROVIDES AN OPPORTUNITY!

So many children find writing a challenge, and that's because they find it hard to construct sentences and they don't have the opportunity to practise. Sentence construction can be challenging, in the same way that long division is super-challenging without a strategy that has been practised many times, over and over again. We dedicate the time to this type of practice in maths, but not in writing. Well that's about to change!

So let's get started. But before we do, I want you to take the following simple idea with you throughout the rest of the book and hopefully into your teaching of writing in the classroom: **Every sentence provides an opportunity!** We want pupils to see every sentence they write as an opportunity to express their skills, abilities and craft in sentence-writing. For pupils to get to this point, we need to embed simple systems to teach, analyse, track and assess, so that all of our pupils can craft a range of core sentences, discuss their grammatical structures and create them independently.

Just like the old saying, 'Look after the pennies, and the pounds will take care of themselves', as teachers we need to, 'Look after the sentences, and the paragraphs will write themselves'.

SOMEBODY PLEASE THINK OF THE ADJECTIVES!

Well it's not quite that dramatic, but it's a fair question. What about the adjectives? It's really simple why they haven't been referenced. This book is all about not being distracted and being able to solely focus on what sentences are and mastering how they are structured. The beauty of the adjective is that it can very easily be added into a sentence to describe without any great difficulty, and is used by most children with ease. Whereas sentence structure is much more complex and needs a dedicated approach and focus, especially for our lower- and middle-ability pupils.

In fact, how often have you, as a teacher, seen poorly structured writing that is full of wonderful adjectives and verbs? We need to switch the narrative and master the sentence first. **Then we can think of the adjectives!**

SENTENCE-LEVEL PROGRESSION

THE PRIMARY NATIONAL CURRICULUM

Let's first take a look at what we are currently working with to guide a sentence-level progression for primary-age pupils – specifically focusing on the content that is genuinely sentence structure or sentence type. We are going to take punctuation and grammar for granted. Inherently, punctuation and grammar make up a huge part of how we structure sentences, but we want to focus specifically on how the curriculum outlines – in a statutory or non-statutory way – how sentences should or might progress throughout our primary National Curriculum.

In the table opposite we have teased out the content that relates directly to sentence structure, which can help us start to map out how sentences might progress across our curriculum. To do this, we have unpicked the 'Composition' and 'Vocabulary, grammar and punctuation' aspects of the Writing Curriculum, and the 'Vocabulary, punctuation and grammar' aspects of the English Appendix 2, focusing on 'Sentence', 'Punctuation' and 'Terminology for pupils', in order to try to piece together the puzzle and highlight what schools are working with when it comes to our precious sentences.

So, this is really as close as the primary National Curriculum gets to referencing and prioritising sentences for our pupils, teachers and schools. The content in Years 1 and 2 briefly mentions sentences. In essence, however, very little instruction is provided in Year 1, apart from in the grammar appendix where the discussion of punctuation alludes to a simple sentence by referencing capital letters and full stops. Year 2 then very quickly moves onto compound and complex sentence structures, including referencing subordination and coordination, but this isn't really mentioned anywhere else.

Once we leave Year 2, the guidance and useful information becomes less and less, the higher up we move through the year groups. As we get to Years 5 and 6, the composition arm of the writing curriculum doesn't have any guidance at all, leaving it to the punctuation and grammar aspect (including Appendix 2) to introduce some more grammatical concepts, such as relative clauses and passive sentence types.

From the information we have, based on our primary National Curriculum, by the end of Year 2, pupils should have really mastered a huge proportion of the sentence structures we want them to be skilled with, ready to apply them in Year 3 and beyond.

From my own personal experience as a teacher and senior leader, this often just isn't the case – for many different reasons. The National Curriculum doesn't really offer much guidance (as outlined) and quite quickly, at a very young age, children (according to the National Curriculum) are expected to have mastered concepts and skills that will, in the real world, need considerable **practice** for them to be made **permanent**. The other worry is that if the curriculum does move on at this pace, and schools have writing policies and progressions mapped against it, then pupils will never be able to catch up.

What we need is a clear, logical and simplified vision for sentences for our pupils and our schools. Let's have a look at what this might look like.

WHAT THE PRIMARY NATIONAL CURRICULUM SAYS ABOUT SENTENCES

Year 1 programme of study

Writing – composition (statutory requirements)
Pupils should be taught to:
• write sentences by:
  – composing a sentence orally before writing it
  – sequencing sentences to form short narratives

Writing – vocabulary, grammar and punctuation (statutory requirements)
Pupils should be taught to:
• develop their understanding of the concepts set out in English Appendix 2 by:
  – joining words and joining clauses using *and*
  – beginning to punctuate sentences using a capital letter and a full stop, question mark or exclamation mark

English Appendix 2: Vocabulary grammar and punctuation **Year 1: Detail of content to be introduced (statutory requirement)** **Sentence** • How **words** can combine to make **sentences** • Joining **words** and joining **clauses** using *and* **Punctuation** • Introduction to capital letters, full stops, question marks and exclamation marks to demarcate **sentences** **Terminology for pupils** • capital letter • sentence • punctuation, full stop, question mark, exclamation mark
Year 2 programme of study
Writing – composition (statutory requirements) Pupils should be taught to: • Consider what they are going to write before beginning by: – encapsulating what they want to say, sentence by sentence

Writing – vocabulary, grammar and punctuation (statutory requirements)
Pupils should be taught to:
• learn how to use:
  – sentences with different forms: statement, question, exclamation, command
  – expanded noun phrases to describe and specify [for example, *the blue butterfly*]
  – subordination (using *when, if, that,* or *because*) and coordination (using *or, and,* or *but*)

English Appendix 2: Vocabulary grammar and punctuation **Year 2: Detail of content to be introduced (statutory requirement)** **Sentence** • **Subordination** (using *when, if, that, because*) and **coordination** (using *or, and, but*) **Punctuation** • Use of capital letters, full stops, question marks and exclamation marks to demarcate **sentences**. **Terminology for pupils** • compound

Year 3 programme of study
Writing – composition (statutory requirements) Pupils should be taught to: • draft and write by: – composing and rehearsing sentences orally (including dialogue), progressively building a varied and rich vocabulary and an increasing range of sentence structures (English Appendix 2)
Writing – vocabulary, grammar and punctuation (statutory requirements) Pupils should be taught to: • develop their understanding of the concepts set out in English Appendix 2 by: – extending the range of sentences with more than one clause by using a wider range of conjunctions, including *when, if, because, although* • using conjunctions, adverbs and prepositions to express time and cause • using fronted adverbials
English Appendix 2: Vocabulary grammar and punctuation **Year 3: Detail of content to be introduced (statutory requirement)** **Sentence** • Expressing time, place and cause using **conjunctions** [for example, *when, before, after, while, so, because*], **adverbs** [for example, *then, next, soon, therefore*], or **prepositions** [for example, *before, after, during, in, because of*] **Punctuation** • *NOTHING RELATED TO SENTENCES* **Terminology for pupils** • conjunction, clause, subordinate clause
Year 4 programme of study
Writing – composition (statutory requirements) *AS FOR YEAR 3 (YEARS 3 AND 4 ARE GROUPED TOGETHER)*
Writing – vocabulary, grammar and punctuation (statutory requirements) *AS FOR YEAR 3 (YEARS 3 AND 4 ARE GROUPED TOGETHER)*
English Appendix 2: Vocabulary grammar and punctuation **Year 4: Detail of content to be introduced (statutory requirement)** **Sentence** • **Fronted adverbials** [for example, <u>*Later that day*</u>, *I heard the bad news.*] **Punctuation** *NOTHING RELATED TO SENTENCES*
Year 5 programme of study
Writing – composition (statutory requirements) *NOTHING RELATED TO SENTENCES*

Writing – vocabulary, grammar and punctuation (statutory requirements)
Pupils should be taught to:
• develop their understanding of the concepts set out in English Appendix 2 by:
  – using expanded noun phrases to convey complicated information concisely
  – using relative clauses beginning with *who, which, where, when, whose, that* or with an implied (i.e. omitted) relative pronoun

English Appendix 2: Vocabulary grammar and punctuation **Year 5: Detail of content to be introduced (statutory requirement)** **Sentence** • Relative clauses beginning with *who, which, where,* when, *whose, that,* or an omitted relative pronoun **Punctuation** • Brackets, dashes or commas to indicate parenthesis • Use of commas to clarify meaning or avoid ambiguity **Terminology** • relative pronoun • relative clause

Year 6 programme of study
Writing – composition (statutory requirements) NOTHING RELATED TO SENTENCES
Writing – vocabulary, grammar and punctuation (statutory requirements) AS FOR YEAR 5 (YEARS 5 AND 6 ARE GROUPED TOGETHER)
English Appendix 2: Vocabulary grammar and punctuation **Year 6: Detail of content to be introduced (statutory requirement)** **Sentence** • Use of the **passive** to affect the presentation of information in a **sentence** [for example, *I broke the window in the greenhouse* versus *The window in the greenhouse was broken (by me)*]. **Punctuation** • Use of the semi-colon, colon and dash to mark the boundary between independent **clauses** [for example, *It's raining; I'm fed up*] **Terminology for pupils** • subject • object • colon • semi-colon

PRIMARY NATIONAL CURRICULUM – SENTENCE CONTENT

We need to start to look at the intent of the curriculum, and the objectives that it alludes to, as the moments these aspects should *start* to be taught, rather than the point by which these objectives should be mastered. If we were learning to play the guitar, we wouldn't learn a chord and then never use it again until we played a song. We would be constantly practising how to play that chord, in conjunction with other chords, over a number of years. There really is no rush, but for some reason in primary education we seem to be in a huge rush to get nowhere.

By seeing the curriculum as a map that navigates our sentence-level journey, we can ensure that every pupil is part of this progressive journey. As teachers, by having a map, we can see where we are, where we have been and where we are going. This map could look like what you see on page 18. The problem, as we have addressed before, is that a lot happens in Years 1 and 2, but then it all seems to fade away, with vague statements and a lack of clarity for teachers and schools. The problem for any children 'working towards' the expected standard in writing is that when they reach Years 3 and 4, the likelihood is that they won't get the practice they need and will remain much further behind, since the curriculum focuses on pretty much everything else other than sentence-level excellence.

The Year 3 and Year 4 periods are a real concern, for all pupils. The curriculum content is too vague, leaves too much to the imagination and makes too many assumptions. From experience, and from speaking to many teachers across the country, nowhere near enough practice happens in these years to ensure pupils reach Years 5, 6 and 7 able to confidently create a range of core sentences.

PRIMARY NATIONAL CURRICULUM – SENTENCE CONTENT

Year Group	Term	Working Towards	Expected	Greater Depth
		Sentence Type Progression		
Year 1	Autumn	Simple Sentence	Simple Sentence	Simple Sentence
Year 1	Spring	Simple Sentence	Simple Sentence	Compound Sentence (and)
Year 1	Summer	Simple Sentence	Compound Sentence (and)	Compound Sentence (and)
Year 2	Autumn	Compound Sentence (and)	Compound Sentence (and)	Compound Sentence – Coordination (and, but, or)
Year 2	Spring	Compound Sentence (and)	Compound Sentence – Coordination (and, but, or)	Complex Sentence Subordination (using when, if, that, because)
Year 2	Summer	Compound Sentence – Coordination (and, but, or)	Complex Sentence Subordination (using when, if, that, because)	
Year 3	Autumn	Compound Sentence – Coordination (and, but, or)	extending the range of sentences with more than one clause by using a wider range of conjunctions, including when, if, because, although (Years 3 and 4)	extending the range of sentences with more than one clause by using a wider range of conjunctions, including when, if, because, although (Years 3 and 4)
Year 3	Spring	Complex Sentence Subordination (using when, if, that, because)		
Year 3	Summer	extending the range of sentences with more than one clause by using a wider range of conjunctions, including when, if, because, although (Years 3 and 4)		
Year 4	Autumn			
Year 4	Spring			
Year 4	Summer			
Year 5	Autumn		Relative Clauses (who, which, where, when, whose, that)	
Year 5	Spring			
Year 5	Summer	Relative Clauses (who, which, where, when, whose, that)		
Year 6	Autumn		Passive Sentences	Semicolon, Colon, Dash Sentences
Year 6	Spring	Passive Sentences		
Year 6	Summer			

SENTENCE NINJA WHOLE-SCHOOL SENTENCE PROGRESSION – OVERVIEW

Let's look at what a whole-school sentence-level progression might look like. But before we dive too deep into the world of sentences, let's remember that what we are trying to do here is create a 'basecamp' for sentences in our school. Later in the book, we will look at some more progressive sentence examples, but the reality is that we need to create a simple and effective system and progression for the core sentence types that all our pupils need to master – their Sentence Ninja Toolkit. As a school, we can then begin the climb up our sentence-level 'Everest'.

The progression table on page 20 outlines what *Sentence Ninja* thinks that sentence-level journey might look like for pupils working towards the expected standard, at the expected standard and at greater depth. This is by no means definitive, but it is certainly simple, clear, logical and achievable. Remember … 'Teaching Simplified, Learning Amplified.'

Schools can develop or adapt this progression in the confidence that all pupils will be equipped with a Sentence Ninja Toolkit of core sentence structures that can be tracked and assessed throughout the school. The beauty of this is that it gives a holistic picture of the whole school's sentence-level capability, allowing for positive action to be taken if pupils are falling behind, on track or even ahead. The fact that we have this knowledge and information means that we can act rather than react, when it's probably already too late.

THE START OF PRACTICE, NOT TEACH AND MOVE ON

Remember, in this model, we are piecing together the information from the 'Composition' and 'Vocabulary, grammar and punctuation' aspects of the Writing Curriculum, and the 'Vocabulary, punctuation and grammar' aspects of the English Appendix 2, focusing on 'Sentence', 'Punctuation' and 'Terminology for pupils' to build a simple progression that works on the premise that this is when each sentence type **starts** being taught and practised from, not taught and forgotten. We want to see a clear progression of 'starting points' where new content is introduced on the sentence-level journey through school.

It's also important to understand this progression for what it is. It's definitely not an assessment tool. What the progression is trying to illustrate is the reality of most classrooms. Some children will naturally learn things much more easily that others, while some children will need more time to consolidate. The beauty is, there is loads of time – six years of it! Six whole years to master seven or eight sentence types and, once pupils have mastered these, they will be able to pretty much write anything they want, in a varied and cohesive fashion. So, regardless of the term, or whether they are working towards the expected standard or at greater depth, the pupils are all on the same journey and will all reach the summit – if we all work towards the same goal.

Sentence Ninja © Andrew Jennings, 2025

Year Group	Term	Working Towards	Expected	Greater Depth
		Sentence Ninja Whole-School Sentence Progression – Overview		
		Sentence Type Progression		
Year 1	Autumn	Simple Sentence	Simple Sentence	Simple Sentence
	Spring	Simple Sentence	Simple Sentence	Compound Sentence (and)
	Summer	Compound Sentence (and)	Compound sentence (and)	Toolkit Milestone 1 *PACE
Year 2	Autumn	Compound Sentence (and)	Toolkit Milestone 1 *PACE	Compound Sentence Coordination (and, but, so)
	Spring	Toolkit Milestone 1 *PACE	Compound Sentence Coordination (and, but, so)	Complex Sentence Subordination (using when, if, because)
	Summer	Compound Sentence Coordination (and, but, so)	Complex Sentence Subordination (using when, if, because)	Toolkit Milestone 2 *PACE
Year 3	Autumn	Compound Sentence Coordination (and, but, so)	Toolkit Milestone 2 *PACE	Compound Sentence Coordination (nor, yet, or, for)
	Spring	Complex Sentence Subordination (using when, if, because)	Compound Sentence Coordination (nor, yet, or, for)	Complex Sentence Subordination (although, while, unless) *however
	Summer	Toolkit Milestone 2 *PACE	Complex Sentence Subordination (although, while, unless) *however	Toolkit Milestone 3 *PACE
Year 4	Autumn	Compound Sentence Coordination (nor, yet, or, for)	Toolkit Milestone 3 *PACE	Procedural Variation 'Create and Connect'
	Spring	Complex Sentence Subordination (although, while, unless) *however	Procedural Variation 'Create and Connect'	Procedural Variation 'Build and Vary'
	Summer	Toolkit Milestone 3 *PACE	Procedural Variation 'Build and Vary'	Toolkit Milestone 4 *PACE
Year 5	Autumn	Procedural Variation 'Create and Connect'	Toolkit Milestone 4 *PACE	Relative Clauses (who, which, that)
	Spring	Toolkit Milestone 4 *PACE	Relative Clauses (who, which, that)	Relative Clauses (where, when, whose)
	Summer	Relative Clauses (who, which, that)	Relative Clauses (where, when, whose)	Embedded Relative Clause
Year 6	Autumn	Relative Clauses (where, when, whose)	Embedded Relative Clause	Toolkit Milestone 5 *PACE
	Spring	Embedded Relative Clause	Toolkit Milestone 5 *PACE	Passive Sentences
	Summer	Toolkit Milestone 5 *PACE	Passive Sentences, Semicolon, Colon, Dash Sentences	Semicolon, Colon, Dash Sentences

*See page 23 for information on PACE.

UNDERSTANDING THE SENTENCE NINJA PROGRESSION

The ultimate aim of the Sentence Ninja Progression is to visualise the sentence-level journey of our pupils throughout primary school. No matter the level a child is working at, if we are working in a committed fashion to practise and progress, then all children should reach Year 6 with a comprehensive and solid sentence-level toolkit, which they can apply in any environment with confidence and skill.

Keep in mind, this is just the foundation that we want to ensure all pupils achieve. It's our minimum commitment to sentence-level competence for all pupils. Remember there are many other grammatical formations, variations and adaptations of sentences that can and will be taught across the rest of the writing curriculum, such as fronted adverbials, for example.

We want a clear system that everyone can look at, understand, and commit to embedding in our classrooms and schools. Remember … 'Teaching Simplified, Learning Amplified'. Essentially we are teaching only three core sentence types: simple sentence, compound sentence and complex sentence, of which the compound and complex sentence structure will have seven variations each, stemming from the conjunctions that will be used within a particular variation. As children move into Years 5 and 6, we will also introduce the relative clause sentence type, which also has six variations, depending on the relative pronoun that is used. Finally, there is the relative embedded clause. So, in total, we will cover 22 clause variations of the three core sentence structures.

To be clear, there are of course more variations and conjunctions that could, and should, be taught within your writing curriculum. What we are doing here is prioritising the most useful ones and those that are the most frequently used. Let's master these 22 variations and equip our pupils with the sentence toolkit that they need.

YEARS 3 AND 4

There's always a lot of hyperbole from primary teachers about how there is often a drop-off from KS1 in Years 3 and 4. Particularly when Year 3 and Year 4 teachers get their hands on KS1 data and there is often a significant disparity between the data and the actual ability of the child, especially in writing.

Let's remember, based on the primary National Curriculum requirements, simple, compound and complex sentences have all been taught by this point and are not individually mentioned again, so if these sentences are not in the child's 'real' toolkit, we have an issue. The lack of specificity around sentences in the Years 3 and 4 curriculum only intensifies this problem over time.

The first thing you hopefully notice about the Sentence Ninja Progression, is that it provides a fluid and natural progression of the core sentence types, and in Years 3 and 4 takes action against this statement: 'Pupils should be taught to: extend[ing] the range of sentences with more than one clause by using a wider range of conjunctions, including *when, if, because, although*' (Writing – vocabulary, grammar and punctuation statutory requirement, Years 3 and 4 programme of study, primary National Curriculum).

This statement, which is supposed to support teachers teach two years of content, is a problem. Yes, as teachers we understand what it's saying, but this statement has really just become a statement on a writing checklist, rather than creating a rich progression of content for schools to thrive off. This really isn't good enough for your wonderful teachers and your amazing pupils.

The Sentence Ninja Progression aims to make Years 3 and 4 the most important years of sentence-level development in primary school, rather than the years that are forgotten.

SENTENCE-LEVEL TOOLKIT – KS1 and KS2

Simple Sentence				
Compound Sentence – **and**	Compound Sentence – **so**	Compound Sentence – **but**	Compound Sentence – **or**	Compound Sentence – **nor**
Compound Sentence – **yet**	Compound Sentence – **for**	Conjunctive Adverb – **however**	Complex Sentence – **when**	
Complex Sentence – **if**	Complex Sentence – **because**	Complex Sentence – **although**	Complex Sentence – **while**	Complex Sentence – **unless**
Relative Clause – **who**	Relative Clause – **which**	Relative Clause – **that**	Relative Clause – **where**	Relative Clause – **when**
Relative Clause – **whose**	Relative Embedded Clause	*do we do bonus sentences – bit more fun for challenge or do we do semicolon, colon, dash	*do we do bonus sentences – bit more fun for challenge or do we do semicolon, colon, dash	*do we do bonus sentences – bit more fun for challenge or do we do semicolon, colon, dash

As you can see in the Whole-School Sentence Progression – Overview (page 20), Years 3 and 4 now explicitly outline which sentence types are introduced, progressed, practised and mastered. The goal of the Year 3/4 period is to bring all pupils to a mastery level for the three core sentences of simple, compound and complex. Ensuring all pupils move effectively into upper KS2, with a high-quality and effective sentence-level toolkit, will mean that they are ready for the writing demands of Years 5 and 6.

It's all simple, but there is a huge amount of knowledge and skill embedded within this toolkit.

SENTENCE TOOLKIT MILESTONES – PACE

Sentence toolkit milestones are simply designed to make us stop and reflect, with each milestone being encompassed by the PACE acronym (see Sentence Ninja Whole-School Sentence Progression – Overview, page 20). This provides an opportunity to dive deeper into the previous terms' content and skills to really ensure that the curriculum doesn't continue to move on without the depth that we really require. This period also allows for additional support for pupils who need more time and support to keep up.

A definition of PACE is as follows:

Practise: Engage in regular exercises or activities to build proficiency in writing basic sentences in a variety of structures.

Apply: Apply newly learned sentences from the previous term(s) in various contexts, genres and micro-activities.

Consolidate: Consolidate learning through teacher modelling, revision and integration of newly acquired skills.

Enable: Empower the child to become more confident in their writing abilities and foster a sense of independence.

This PACE time period is extremely valuable and allows everyone who is involved in the process (SLT, teacher, TA and pupil) to fully understand and consolidate where the pupil is on their sentence-level journey (see page 107 for suggested activities).

PACE PROGRESSION

PACE Milestone 1 – Simple sentences and compound sentence (and).

PACE Milestone 2 – Compound sentences (and, but, so), complex sentences (when, if, because).

PACE Milestone 3 – Compound sentences (nor, yet, so, for), complex sentences (although, while, unless), conjunctive adverb (however).

PACE Milestone 4 – All simple, compound and complex sentences.

PACE Milestone 5 – Relative and embedded clauses.

Within the Years 3 and 4 Sentence Ninja Whole-School Sentence Progression – Overview (page 20), you may have noticed the terms that are dedicated to 'Procedural Variation'. These periods are the final stages of our pupils mastering the three core sentence types and applying their knowledge and sentence-level skill. Once again, it's important to note that this is an extremely high-value and highly specified period of time where pupils will deepen their understanding ready for upper KS2.

PROCEDURAL VARIATION – CREATE AND CONNECT

The Create and Connect period (see page 20) is all about bringing together everything that Year 4 pupils have learned over the past three years in order to craft sentences and connect ideas together, through the use of a variety of clause structures with a range of conjunctions and punctuation. This is a time to allow pupils to develop their ability to be creative with their sentences, while allowing time to discuss the meaning and impact of the structure of the sentence and its components. Ultimately, the 'Create and Connect' period is very much about pupils having a huge number of opportunities to practise connecting their ideas effectively within many different scenarios, activities and tasks. Find 'Create and Connect' tasks on page 126.

PROCEDURAL VARIATION – BUILD AND VARY

Build and Vary (see page 20) provides opportunities for Year 4 pupils to develop high-quality passages of writing that focus on sentence-level variation and clause variation, which will support coherence within a paragraph. These activities will be even more independent than the 'Create and Connect' period, allowing for pupils to really demonstrate their core sentence competency. During the 'Build and Vary' period, we want pupils to realise that if they can develop varied paragraph size content, ultimately it's very much just a case of write and repeat to create larger writing outcomes, using their Sentence Ninja Toolkit. Find 'Build and Vary' tasks on page 131.

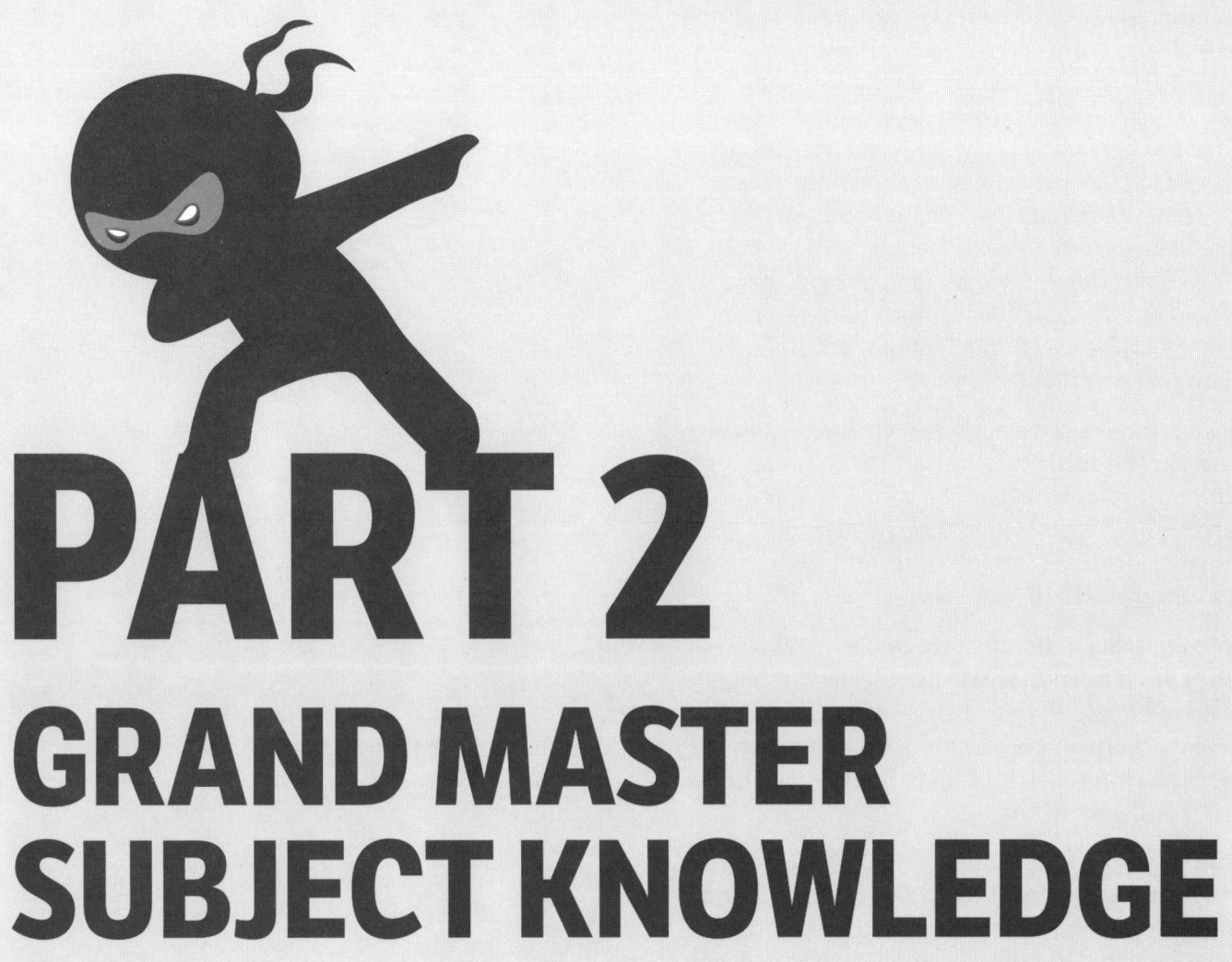

PART 2
GRAND MASTER SUBJECT KNOWLEDGE

ESSENTIAL SUBJECT KNOWLEDGE

The key ingredient to ensuring we can embed a simple and effective progression within our classroom or school, is to ensure we have the key subject knowledge that we require to teach sentences extremely well. As stated at the beginning of the book, we need all staff and pupils to be able to effectively and simply state what a sentence is and what constitutes a sentence. Everyone needs to be crystal clear on this right from day one, as this simple knowledge is going to become part of everyday teaching and interaction with pupils, from Year 1 all the way through until Year 6. This is a constant non-negotiable.

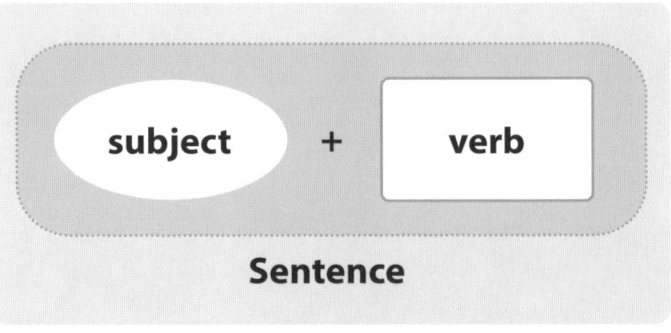

We have formed a sentence when we have a **subject** and a **verb**. The **subject** is the part of the sentence that describes the '**who**' and the verb is the '**action**' that the subject is performing. We need both grammatical features (subject and verb) if we are to form a sentence. It's that simple.

Notice in this illustration that the subject is circled and the verb is boxed. We will use these two shapes – oval and rectangle – when exploring the subject and verbs in tasks and in our teaching. This is an extremely simple visual approach for staff to implement and for pupils to understand and apply.

In order to ensure that children and staff are not just able to recite what constitutes a sentence – with no real understanding – we must make the sentence part of our everyday dialogue and daily practice with our pupils, so we are constantly asking, probing, questioning, modelling, showing and exploring the subject and verb. In so doing, this will mean that pupils are very clear, in a range of different scenarios and situations, what a sentence actually is and what it is made up of. Once we have established this, writing and punctuating sentences becomes a whole lot easier! And, let's not forget, this is the first sentence type we are looking to master within our toolkit. By forming a sentence with a subject and a verb, we have formed a simple sentence.

Sentence-Level Subject Knowledge Disclaimer

Even at this early point, it's important just to highlight a few points about the wider grammatical picture. Although not referenced in the primary National Curriculum, the **predicate** is the more complex version of exploring and understanding the 'verb form' within a sentence. The predicate encompasses the other words within the sentence that describes the action. The predicate will always include a verb.

All of the sentences we will explore and prioritise will be made up of other features. The reason for not covering these aspects in any detail within this book is that these features, variations, phrases and forms within sentence structure and grammar can be potentially endless and should really become part of the wider English curriculum. Right now, our aim isn't to cover all of the grammar associated with sentences; rather, we are trying to ensure you finish reading this book with the simplest and most powerful pieces of information that will put you and your pupils on the track to sentence-level success.

Once pupils have a strong and real understanding of the subject and the verb, knowing how and when to punctuate a sentence with a full stop is a much more concrete and real skill. It gets us away from horrible phrases like 'a sentence is a complete thought or idea' which is beyond abstract and completely unhelpful. It's phrases like this that contribute to a lack of understanding for pupils, borne out of a lack of clarity from staff around grammatical subject knowledge. Believe me, I've been there!

What else should we know about a sentence? You may have heard the word 'clause', but how does it relate to a sentence? Well, quite simply, if we have a subject and a verb, then we have a clause. If we decide to house the clause within a capital letter and full stop, then the clause is a sentence. Just because we have a clause doesn't mean we have a sentence; how we punctuate the clause determines this. So, when punctuated as a simple sentence, then we have a main or independent clause, which is the correct way of understanding the other horrible sentence phrase of 'if it makes sense on its own it's a sentence' … another teaching classic, borne out of poor subject knowledge.

It makes sense on its own because it has a subject and a verb. It's crucial that children understand that this simple sentence is an independent/main clause (they are the same thing – some schools have preferred ways of referring to this) because this clause structure will be used again within compound and complex sentences. So, understanding that a simple sentence, which contains a subject and a verb, is an independent/main clause is very important.

In both your own classroom and the whole school, you need to ensure there is a consistent and very simple explanation of what a sentence is. This should ensure that everyone can articulate not only what a sentence is, but can also identify both the subject and verb in sentences, and can create sentences with a subject and a verb. Pupils should also be able to signal what the subject and verb is in all of these situations. (See subject and verb tasks on page 28.) For example, within a simple sentence like below, which many Year 1 pupils might write, the sentence is made up of a (subject), a [verb] and an (object).

(Alex) [ran] to the (park).

'Alex' is the subject, 'ran' is the verb and 'park' is the object. To decide the 'who' (Alex or the park), we need to ask, 'who' ran? Alex ran, so Alex is the subject, park is the object. At a young age we don't want to dive into the grammatical wormholes that should really be introduced at a much older age, but children should be consistently exposed to the concept of the subject and the verb right from the start of building sentences. Even with just subtle sentence variations, such as adding the odd word here or there, the grammatical features and conventions grow in complexity very quickly.

As an aside, in the 'Vocabulary, grammar and punctuation' section of Appendix 2 of the primary National Curriculum, 'subject' is first referenced in Year 6, and 'verb' is referenced in Year 2, which is interesting when written sentence structure starts in Year 1. We have already explored the potential flaws of the National Curriculum when it comes to sentence-level clarity, so it's not surprising that it could be argued that the importance of the associated grammar isn't aligned. However, what we must agree on is the importance of teaching and building this core understanding right from the start.

SUBJECT AND VERB EXAMPLES

Below are some examples of fairly simple sentences that highlight the subject and the verb. Even in writing these simple sentences, the thought process to ensure clarity wasn't straightforward, which just highlights how pupils need to be exposed to sentences as much as possible so they can become comfortable and familiar with subject and verb.

Staff and pupils should be able to begin to look at **all sentences** that they encounter and analyse/ask, 'Which is the subject and which is the verb?' It should be a relentless and constant process undertaken by everyone.

The (duck) [quacked].

(Mia) [threw] the ball.

My (friend) [likes] cheeseburgers.

Can (we) [visit] the fair?

The (car) [zoomed] past the school.

A note on modal and auxiliary verbs

As sentences become more advanced, they will contain modal verbs (verbs indicating possibility or necessity, such as 'could' and 'should'), and auxiliary verbs (helping verbs, such as 'was' and 'had'), which help the main verb within the sentence to function. For the purposes of this book, we are focusing solely on the main verb.

PHOTOCOPIABLE ACTIVITIES – SUBJECT AND VERB

The aim of the activities below is to provide regular opportunities for teachers and pupils to question, answer, explore and identify the subject and verb in simple sentences. Each activity's goal is the same; to provide sentence-level examples whereby the teacher and pupil need to discuss and identify the subject and the main verb of the sentence.

Subject Strip Circle the subject in each sentence.	**Verb Strip** Draw a rectangle around the verb in each sentence.
The birds collected seeds.	Freddy jumped on the bed.
My puppy chewed the blanket.	Marcus ate his yummy pizza.
A person was at the door.	Collect your rubbish, please.
We must visit the library.	I watched the film.
Samiha drew a picture.	Shall we rest on the bench?
The coffee was very hot.	I charged my phone battery.
Every meal was tasty.	Mia cleaned her bedroom.
Dad rode his bike to work.	The cat purred at its owner.
The children played on the swings.	The heavy rain bounced off the floor.
Mary was very happy today.	Mum poured Shelly some milk.

PHOTOCOPIABLE ACTIVITIES – SUBJECT AND VERB

Similar to the previous activity, pupils still need to focus on the subject and verb separately, but this time they are adding in an appropriate subject or verb to enable the sentence to function.

Subject Strip
Fill in the gap in each sentence with a subject.

The _____ visited the museum.

_____ cut her knee.

A _____ played in the garden.

_____ wore our football kit.

_____ cracked his new tablet.

The _____ was closed.

_____ didn't like to share.

The _____ was cancelled.

_____ bought some sweets.

A _____ walked past.

Verb Strip
Fill in the gap in each sentence with a verb.

Dad was _____.

A bird _____ over my head.

I _____ my pencil.

Arnold is _____ on the bench.

I _____ the questions.

Monty _____ a cake.

The dog _____ loudly.

We _____ the seaside.

I _____ the book.

Mia _____ her biscuits.

Sentence Ninja © Andrew Jennings, 2025

PHOTOCOPIABLE ACTIVITIES – SUBJECT AND VERB

Pupils will now need the opportunity to look at simple sentences and identify the subject and the main verb found within each. Ask pupils to show the subject by circling it and the verb by drawing a rectangle around it.

Simple Sentence – Activity 1
Circle the subject and draw a rectangle around the verb.

The dog was sleeping.	Dani tripped on the rock.
Mia licked the ice cream.	Mr Crooks read a book.
A car crashed into a wall.	The family visited the park.
She played on the swings.	Joseph washed his face.
My teddy fell onto the floor.	Shane kicked the ball.
Sami used his spoon.	Mum paid for lunch.

Simple Sentence – Activity 2
Circle the subject and draw a rectangle around the verb.

A red car drove past my house.	Everyone came for a walk.
The fierce lion roared.	The cold rain hurt my face.
Yellow flowers danced in the wind.	Sam was late for school again.
I heard the fire alarm.	We collected litter from our area.
Jan shared his sweets with me.	Brave firefighters came to help.
The fluffy cat purred next to me.	The bright light created a shadow.

Simple Sentence – Activity 3
Circle the subject and draw a rectangle around the verb.

The old oak tree creaked in the wind.	Merlin cast a protection spell.
My door slammed shut.	Freddy pushed past Anwar.
The berries tasted very sweet.	The sirens echoed for miles.
Dad wanted to watch the football.	John winked slyly to his friends.
Our car was covered in mud.	Sophie studied modern dance.
The cheeky squirrel stole the nuts.	Green flies buzzed all around us.

PHOTOCOPIABLE ACTIVITIES – SUBJECT AND VERB

This activity resembles a SATs-style grammar question, where pupils are asked to identify the subject and the main verb in each sentence by adding an 'S' for the subject and a 'V' for the verb.

Put an S in the box underneath the subject and a V in the box underneath the verb.

The naughty children looked through the dusty window.

☐ ☐ ☐ ☐ ☐ ☐

Put an S in the box underneath the subject and a V in the box underneath the verb.

The beautiful princess escaped from the tower.

☐ ☐ ☐ ☐ ☐ ☐

Put an S in the box underneath the subject and a V in the box underneath the verb.

I slowly climbed the terrifying, rocky mountain.

☐ ☐ ☐ ☐ ☐

Put an S in the box underneath the subject and a V in the box underneath the verb.

In the distance, a fearsome lion hid in the savannah grass.

☐ ☐ ☐ ☐ ☐

Put an S in the box underneath the subject and a V in the box underneath the verb.

Mr Boddington carefully turned the page of the book.

☐ ☐ ☐ ☐ ☐

Sentence Ninja © Andrew Jennings, 2025

PHOTOCOPIABLE ACTIVITIES – SUBJECT AND VERB

When pupils are comfortable with the concept and structure of a compound sentence, we can start to regularly explore subjects and verbs within them. Use these activities to explore the subject and main verb within each clause of a compound sentence with coordinating conjunctions.

Compound Sentence – Activity 1

Circle each subject and draw a rectangle around each verb in the sentences below.

Clause	Conjunction	Clause
The girls went to the park,	but	the boys visited the beach.
Amy kicked the ball over the fence,	so	Jenny jumped over to get it.
Birds hunted for worms,	and	bees buzzed around the garden.
Should Mia enter the forest,	or	should she walk through the swamp?
The music sounded very loud,	yet	no one minded.
Andrew didn't like the cold snow,	nor	did he want to go for a walk in it.
The lunch box was full,	so	Paul ate as much as he could.

Compound Sentence – Activity 2

Circle each subject and draw a rectangle around each verb in the sentences below.

Clause	Conjunction	Clause
The swings were broken,	but	the children had fun anyway.
Steph tidied her bedroom,	so	her friends could play.
The trees bent in the wind,	and	leaves danced on the ground.
Do I eat the chocolate bar now,	or	do I save it for later?
The alarm was ringing loudly,	yet	no one moved at all.
He didn't listen to the advice,	nor	did he revise for the test.
The soup was very hot,	so	Dan ate the sandwich instead.

PHOTOCOPIABLE ACTIVITIES – SUBJECT AND VERB

This activity requires pupils to understand that in a short passage of text, every sentence must contain a subject and a verb. Each activity is made up of three sentences with a mix of simple and compound sentences. Pupils should circle the subject and draw a rectangle around the main verb.

Circle each subject and draw a rectangle around each verb in the sentences below.

Mia decided to play with her friends. They kicked a football and they played on the swings. The girls loved the sun.

Circle each subject and draw a rectangle around each verb in the sentences below.

The fox sneaked slowly from the bushes and moved closer to a picnic. The picnic smelled so good. The fox licked her lips, yet she knew it would be difficult to get the food.

Circle each subject and draw a rectangle around each verb in the sentences below.

It was snowing outside, so Kara decided to build a snowman. The snow fell harder and harder. The snow covered Kara's face. The snowman grew taller, and Kara added eyes and a nose.

Circle each subject and draw a rectangle around each verb in the sentences below.

Daniel sat in the maths lesson, and he listened carefully to Mrs Francis. The lesson focused on different triangles. Daniel thought it was quite easy, yet his friend found it hard.

Circle each subject and draw a rectangle around each verb in the sentences below.

The children went to the dinosaur museum on a coach. Mr Moon knew lots about dinosaurs, so he led the tour. Everyone learned a lot of facts, and some children wanted to come again.

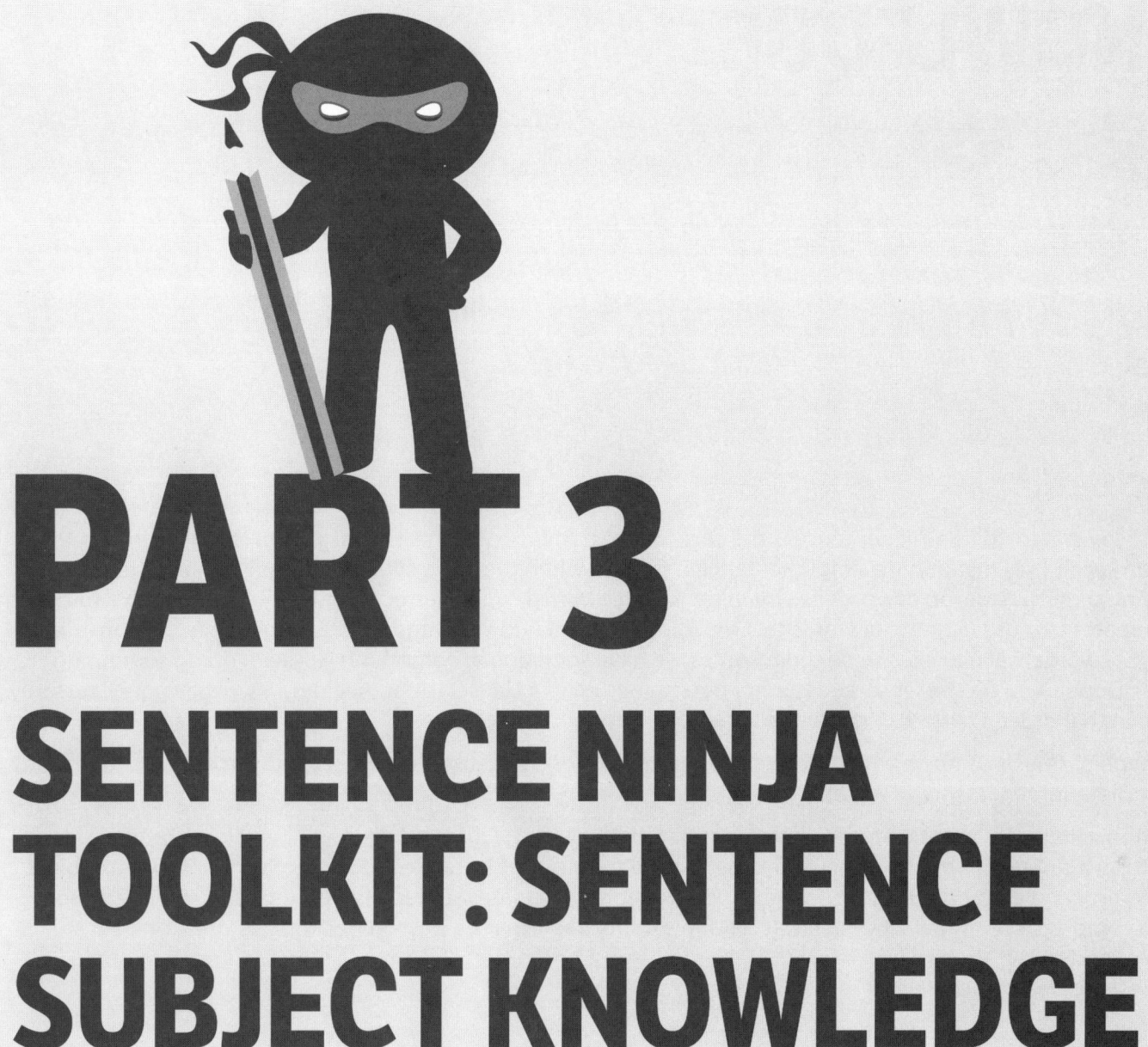

PART 3
SENTENCE NINJA TOOLKIT: SENTENCE SUBJECT KNOWLEDGE

ESSENTIAL SUBJECT KNOWLEDGE

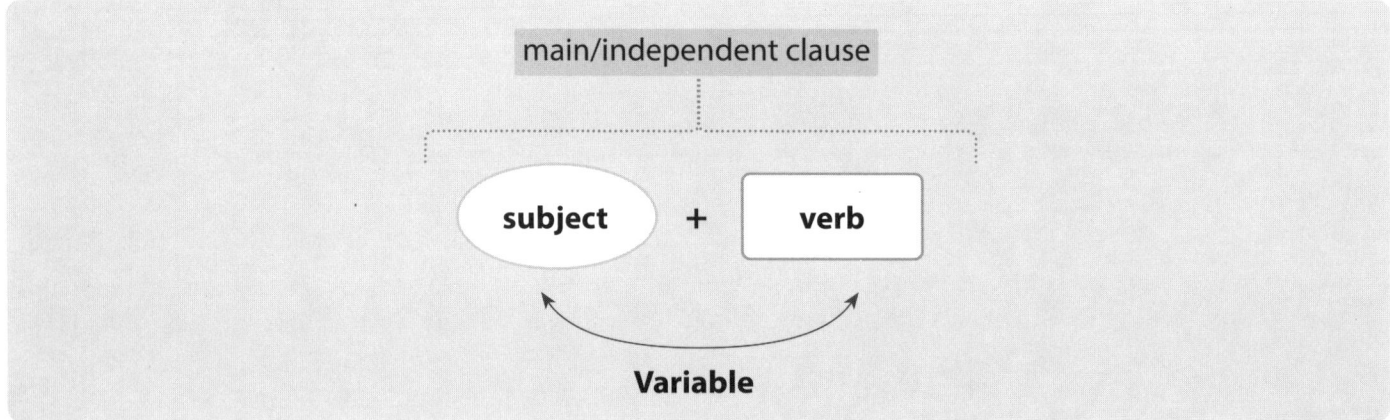

As already stated, the simple sentence is the core foundation from which all other sentences will stem. As we can see in the illustration, a simple sentence is formed when there is a subject and a verb, and when the beginning of these group of words has been punctuated with a capital letter and the end closed with a full stop. This creates a clause (a group of words that includes a subject and verb) and, because there is a full stop, this group of words 'will make sense on their own' as we have someone or something (subject) doing something (verb). Depending on the tense, structure or passive nature of a clause, the subject and verb may not necessarily come in that order. The verb might actually come before the subject.

This type of clause is known as an independent or main clause, because the subject and verb allow us to create a complete sentence, should we wish.

It's important at this point that we understand that as pupils write, they will create phrases (groups of words that form a single unit but cannot function as complete sentences because they do not contain **both** a subject and a verb) and clauses, but it is their use of punctuation that creates sentences. Sentences, as they become more complex, may contain multiple clauses. If we understand that a clause in its simplest form contains a subject and a verb, then we can really start to understand how different sentence structures, with multiple clauses, are created accurately.

EXAMPLES OF CLAUSES

Paul shouted over to Daniel.	A bird landed on the grass.
Should we swim in the river?	The rain poured all day long.
The team won the game.	Can I help?
She opened the door carefully.	The toast was burnt.

We want children to be aware of when they have created a clause (and how simple it is), and that they can punctuate it with a full stop to create a simple sentence. Children having complete understanding of this very simple concept is extremely powerful.

EXAMPLES OF CLAUSES FOR SELF-ANALYSIS AND DISCUSSION

Mary filled her cup.	Hamza read her book.
The dog barked at the visitor.	Today we visited London.
We ran home.	Charlie grazed his knee.
I need the toilet.	The class were noisy.

Let's not forget all the other wonderful grammatical features that you'll teach our young writers, such as adjectives, expanded noun phrases, adverbs and so on. All of these can be housed within the simple sentence, adding detail to the subject and the verb.

A note on modal and auxiliary verbs

As sentences become more advanced, they will contain modal verbs (verbs indicating possibility or necessity, such as 'could' and 'should'), and auxiliary verbs (helping verbs, such as 'was' and 'had'), which help the main verb within the sentence to function. For the purposes of this book, we are focusing solely on the main verb.

COMPOUND SENTENCES

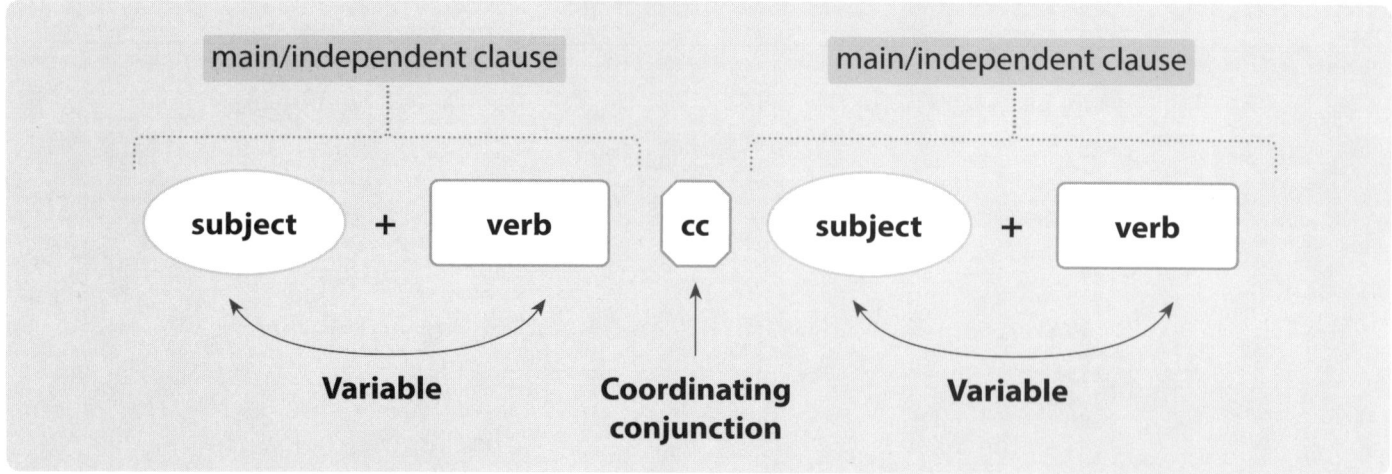

The compound sentence is actually quite exciting. Exciting because it is really easy to understand how it functions, now that we understand the simple sentence and its nature as a clause (subject and verb). What is even more exciting is, whereas so far we have added only one sentence (maybe the most important) to our sentence toolkit, with the compound sentence we are adding seven more!

Hopefully, you've already looked at the illustration of the compound sentence and have put it together yourself, but before we dive into the sentence type, let's explore the word 'compound'. The Oxford English Dictionary defines compound as 'a thing composed of two or more separate elements'. So, essentially, a compound sentence is a sentence that is made up of several parts; in the example above, two – two clauses. And we know what a clause is from our time with the simple sentence.

So, a compound sentence is just two or more separate clauses that are main/independent clauses – meaning 'they make sense on their own', because they have a subject and a verb and could both be punctuated to form a simple sentence. But, in the compound sentence, we join these clauses together using a coordinating conjunction. So, either side of the coordinating conjunction, we would have a subject and a verb.

But where do we get seven different sentence types from? Well, the coordinating conjunction is our secret weapon because there are seven coordinating conjunctions we can use to convey a different meaning within the same structure. These conjunctions are commonly referred to using the acronym FANBOYS.

For And Nor But Or Yet So

Each conjunction has a different meaning and performs a different role – but they all need to be used accurately.

MISCONCEPTIONS ABOUT COORDINATING CONJUNCTIONS

Acronyms, such as FANBOYS, are extremely popular in education, but there is a real danger with them. I think for the purpose of remembering all seven conjunctions, an acronym is useful, but the prevalence of the acronym has the power to dilute children's and teachers' understanding of the conjunctions themselves. I've experienced this first hand in many settings. SATs are probably the main culprit for needing to recall conjunctions rapidly, rather than promoting the need to develop a real understanding of what conjunctions are and how they function.

Another minor misconception I find is around the use of 'and'. Although 'and' is an extremely common word in writing, using 'and' doesn't automatically mean we have formed a compound sentence.

For example:

The dog barked at the cat *and* noisy birds.

Above we have a (main) clause, as we have a subject and verb. We then have the coordinating conjunction 'and' followed by 'noisy birds', which is an adjective and a subject. So we have a phrase, not a clause. This sentence is absolutely fine, but it is a simple sentence. It just comes back to whether the subject and verb are present. Simple. Essentially, 'and' is just listing the cat and the birds. This use of 'and' is a misconception for pupils that I'd suggest is borne out of the superficial use of FANBOYS to gloss over the actual structure and understanding of a sentence.

Can your pupils explain what each coordinating conjunction does? Well, they need to be able to. The sentence-level void in the Years 3 and 4 curriculum only compounds this issue, when this should really be the perfect time for pupils to master their understanding of these wonderful conjunctions. If children don't understand the power of each conjunction, how can we expect them to use them with skill to create different sentence types?

MODERATION FEEDBACK

From my own experience of whole-school, cross-academy and local authority moderation, varied compound sentences with varied conjunctions are one of the main writing features that start to disappear for middle-ability writers, especially as they reach Years 5 and 6. The comma and complex sentences seem to dominate. I propose it's more likely that children don't use conjunctions effectively because they don't really understand them. So let's help pupils to understand them better. See pages 40–43 to explore each coordinating conjunction, understand their meanings and see some examples.

EXAMPLES OF COMPOUND SENTENCES USING COORDINATING CONJUNCTIONS

Freddy ran to see the cow, **and** Jenny watched from the car.	Imran knew he needed to leave, **yet** he couldn't take a step.
Tom wanted to go to the cinema, **but** Mia wanted to go bowling.	Freya didn't know where she was, **nor** did she remember how to get home.
The bird landed on the branch, **so** it could watch for worms.	Karl went to the store, **for** he needed ingredients for the soup.
They could go to the beach, **or** they could visit their cousin.	We hid in the shadows, **and** we held our breaths.

Understanding the importance of the subject and the verb can really help pupils to structure genuine compound sentences.

EXAMPLES OF COMPOUND SENTENCES USING COORDINATING CONJUNCTIONS FOR SELF-ANALYSIS AND DISCUSSION

The werewolf howled under the moon, and bats scurried through the mist.	Danny was hurt, yet he wanted to continue.
Francis was making his bed, but he was distracted by his sister.	Rio had not finished the test, nor had Chen.
They all waited by the window, so they could see Mr Hand's car.	The gang all cheered, for Henry had completed the challenge.
Should we eat pasta, or could we eat pizza instead?	Tom cried, and Mia wailed.

COORDINATING CONJUNCTIONS – MEANINGS AND FUNCTION

The importance of conjunctions cannot be underestimated. On the following pages, we will explore each conjunction, its variation and how we should teach it. The explanations provided are aimed at the pupils, to really simplify in our minds what we are trying to accomplish by using each conjunction.

The task of teaching coordinating conjunctions is potentially made even easier by focusing on those that are most high frequency. In most children's writing, 'and', 'but', 'so', 'or' and 'yet' will be the most encountered, most read and most functional conjunctions. 'Nor' and 'for' are likely to be used less frequently, although they should still be taught.

Remember, the explanations on the following pages have been kept super simple, so that you and your pupils can use these phrases consistently in school.

AND

Essential Explanation: 'and' joins two clauses together.

Example: The wolf wandered to the river, **and** it watched the moon rise.

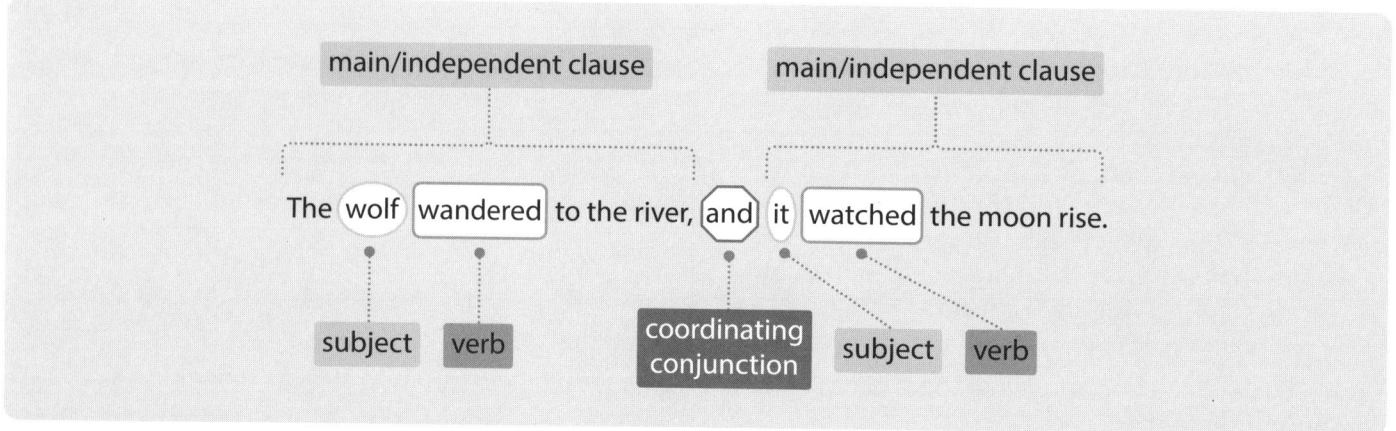

Sentence Context:

'**and**', when used properly, is a highly effective tool for joining and sequencing ideas. Children who run on with sentences without much thought of punctuation would benefit hugely from mastering the use of 'and' to build a compound sentence. It is also a high-frequency coordinating conjunction, so mastering 'and' is essential for all pupils … and teachers. In addition to joining two clauses together, 'and' can also join individual words and phrases – for example, 'bread and butter' or 'soft bread and creamy butter'.

BUT

Essential Explanation: 'but' contrasts two clauses.

Example: Merlin wanted to cast a spell, **but** Arthur thought it was too dangerous.

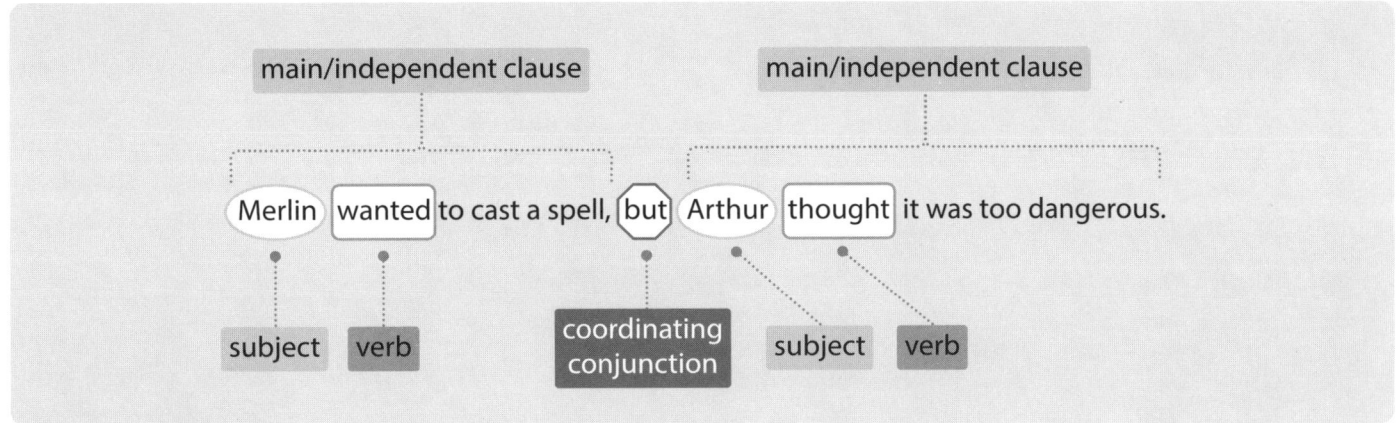

Sentence Context:

'**but**' is another wonderful sentence tool for pupils, when they genuinely understand what the conjunction does. The word contrast might be tricky for pupils to grasp, so we can help them understand in the early stages by explaining how 'but' shows a **great difference**, an opposition or an **opposite thought or stance** on an issue. The more examples pupils see, the more they will understand what 'contrast' actually means.

OR

Essential Explanation: 'or' joins two clauses to show two options, alternatives or possibilities.

Example: Should Mia eat beans on toast, **or** should she eat pepperoni pizza?

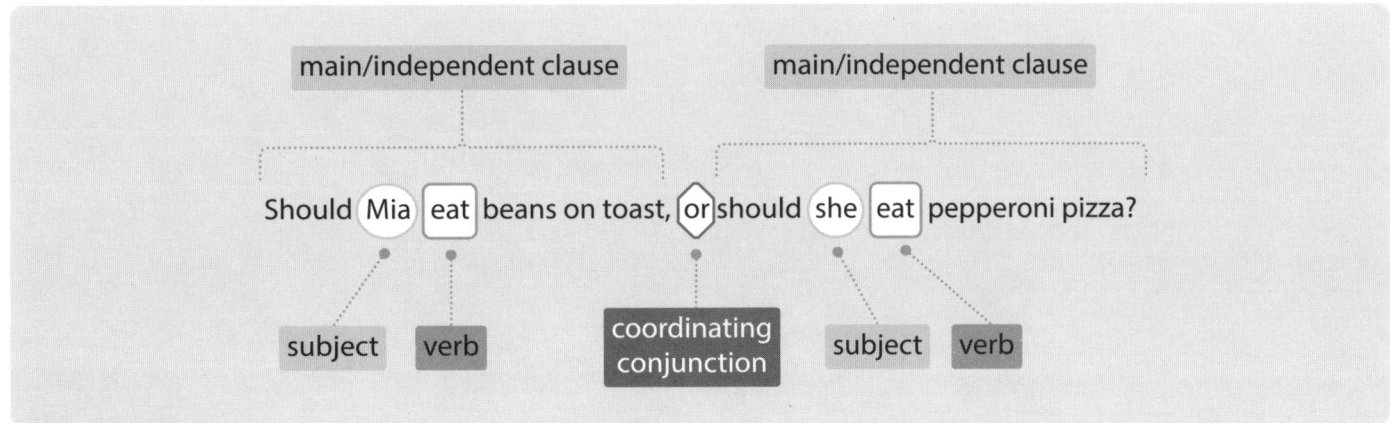

Sentence Context:

'**or**' is one of the simpler conjunctions to understand as it joins two ideas – a bit like 'and' – and lets the writer show two options. This conjunction can often be used with modal verbs to enhance the suggestion of likelihood or possibility, which is another feature children need to be able to demonstrate.

SO

Essential Explanation: 'so' is used to show the result or the 'why?' of the first clause.

Example: Andrew saved all of his money, **so** that he could buy his family a gift.

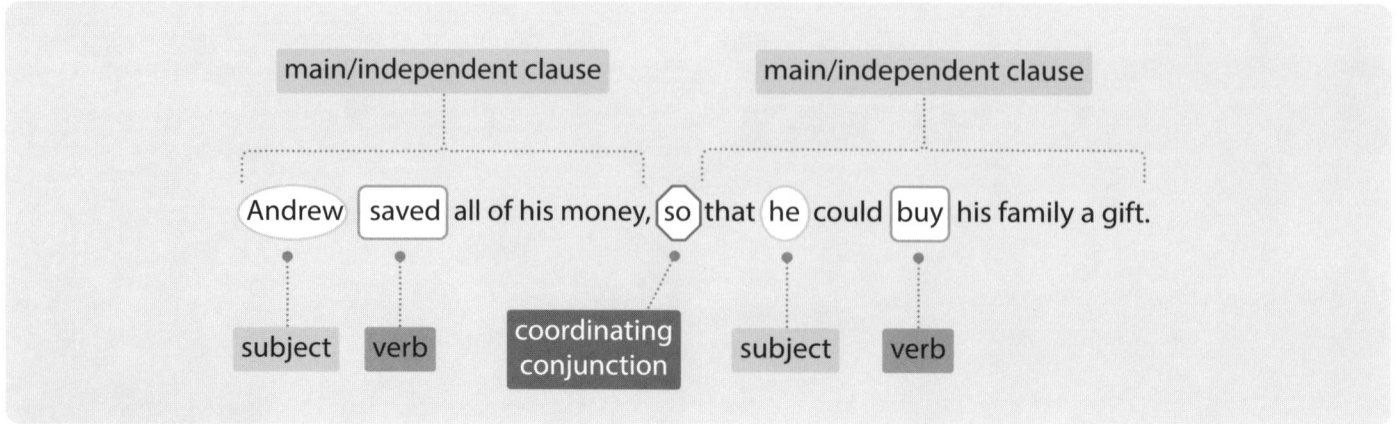

Sentence Context:

'**so**' is a great sentence tool to have in our toolkit. It can be easily explained to pupils by likening 'so' to 'because', as it produces a very similar outcome. For example:

Andrew saved all of his money, because he wanted to buy his family a gift.

So is great for explaining 'why?'. 'Why' did Andrew save his money? 'So' he could buy his family a gift. '**So**' can help us dive into the thoughts and motivations of a character.

YET

Essential Explanation: '**yet**' contrasts two clauses, in a similar way to 'but'.

Example: Mary loved playing football matches, **yet** she hated training sessions.

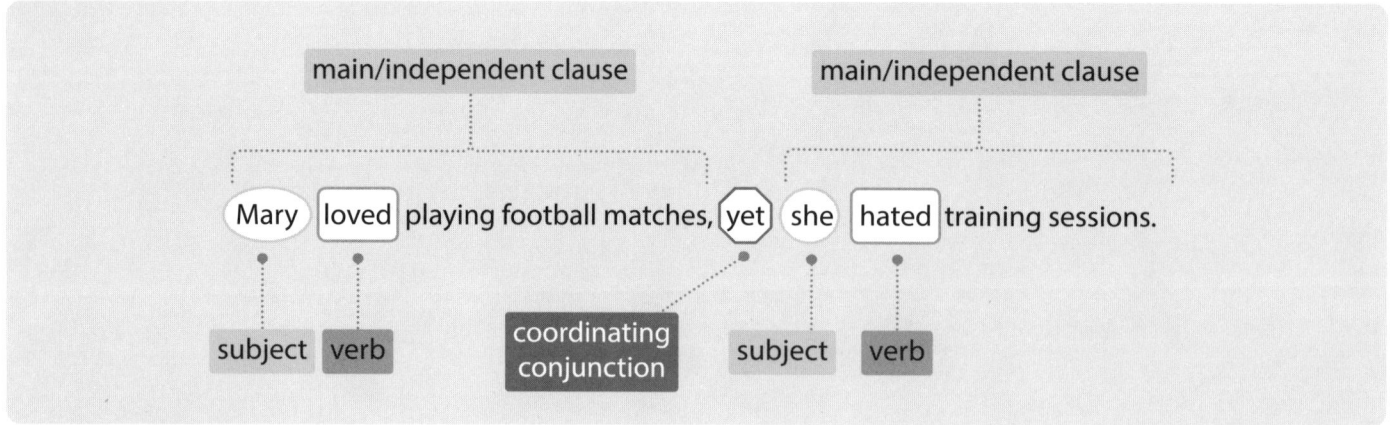

Sentence Context:

'**yet**' should be pretty easy to add to our sentence-level toolkit as it performs exactly the same job as 'but' – it offers a contrast, but with a subtle difference. '**Yet**' is slightly more formal than 'but' and suggests a stronger contrast. It is so strong, that it has a hint or suggestion of surprise, mystery or expectation. In the example, it is a little surprising that someone loving football matches really hates training sessions. Love and hate are a significant and strong contrast.

NOR

Essential Explanation: 'nor' joins two negative clauses.

Example: They hadn't vanquished the dragon, **nor** had they found the prisoners.

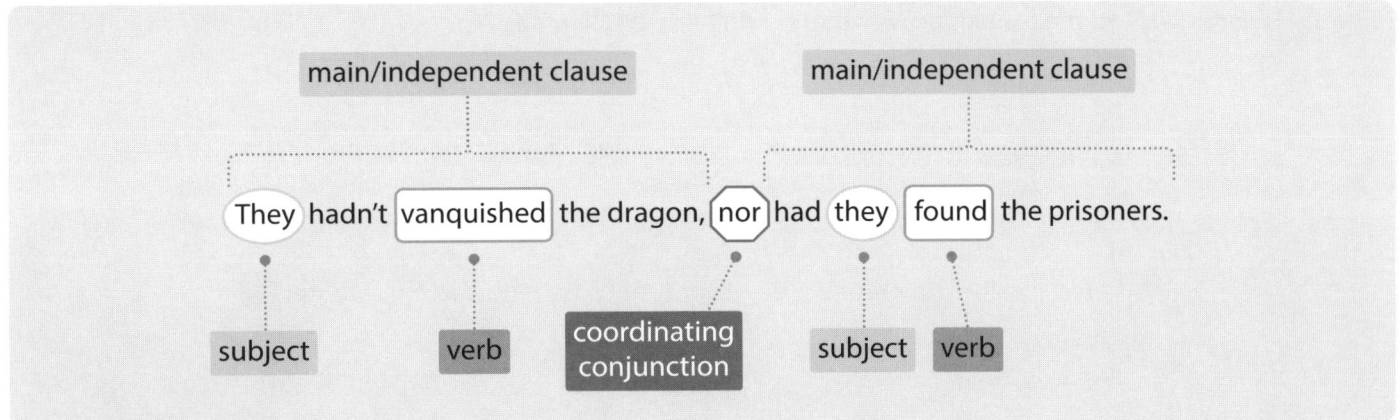

Sentence Context:

'**nor**' is one of the less common conjunctions, but it can still be an effective tool in our sentence-level arsenal! The first clause needs to be negative (in the example, '**hadn't vanquished**'), then we can use '**nor**' to add a further negative clause. With practice, '**nor**' can be mastered easily and can add real complexity to pupils' writing.

FOR

Essential Explanation: '**for**' explains 'why' (in a similar way to 'because').

Example: We must recycle all plastic, **for** the planet depends on it.

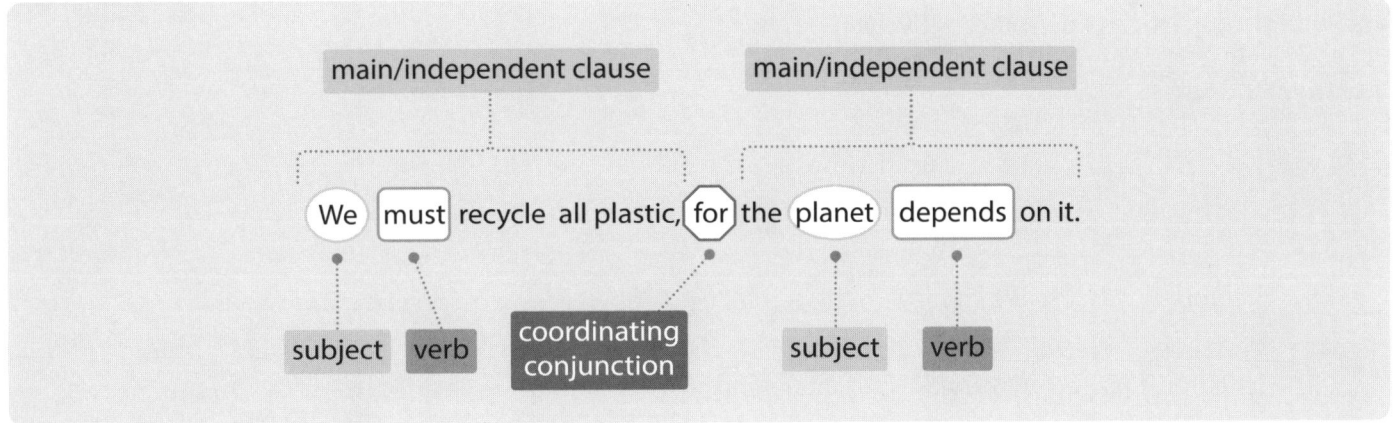

Sentence Context:

'**for**' is probably our least frequently used coordinating conjunction. It's less common and more formal than 'because', but if we think about how it is very similar to 'because', we can start to understand how and when to use it. Again, knowing '**for**' is similar to 'because' can help us structure sentences and provide variety via the conjunction, especially in more formal writing outcomes. This might be a persuasive letter, balanced argument or even an historical diary entry where '**for**' provides high value.

SENTENCE-LEVEL OPTIONAL EXTRA
HOWEVER

Essential Explanation: 'however' shows a contrast or contradiction (in a similar way to 'but').

Example: Pablo visited the funfair; **however**, he didn't ride a rollercoaster.

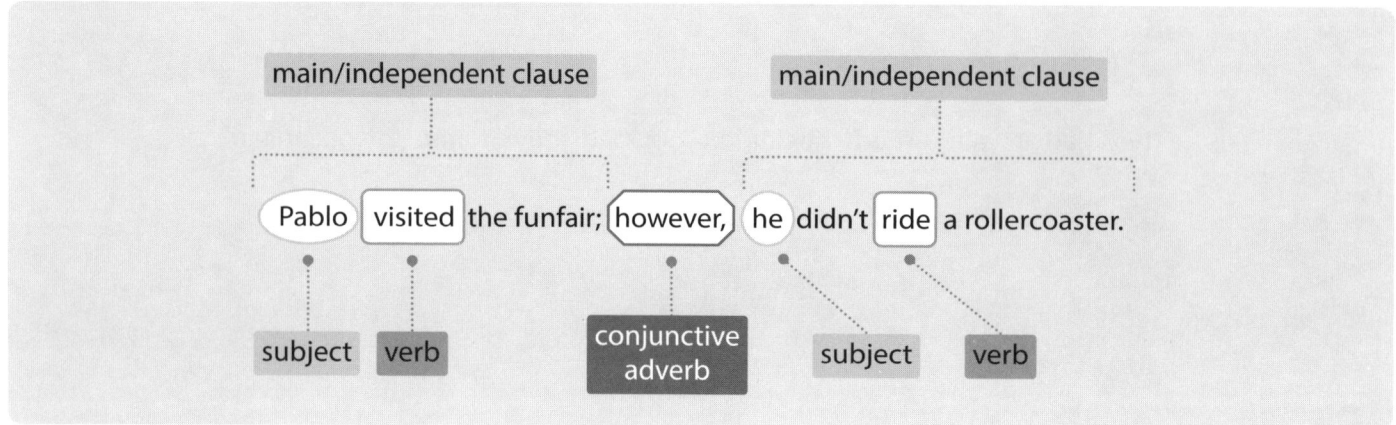

Sentence Context:

The first important thing to note here is that '**however**' is not a coordinating conjunction, nor is it a subordinating conjunction (a word that connects an independent clause with a dependent/subordinate clause that provides extra information). It is a conjunctive adverb, and it is not joining the clauses together like a conjunction does. Instead, its job is to show a relationship between two **independent clauses** and to transition from one idea to the next. That's why it has been included in this section, due to the inclusion of two independent clauses. So, 'however' is more of a cohesive device than it is a grammatical feature. Nonetheless, it is still extremely effective in helping us build a sentence with a multifaceted structure with high-level punctuation. And, best of all, it is really simple to structure a sentence using '**however**'. After the first clause, we simply use a semicolon, followed by '**however**', then we add a comma before the next clause. It's really simple, and with practice it can be used effectively.

Further Examples:

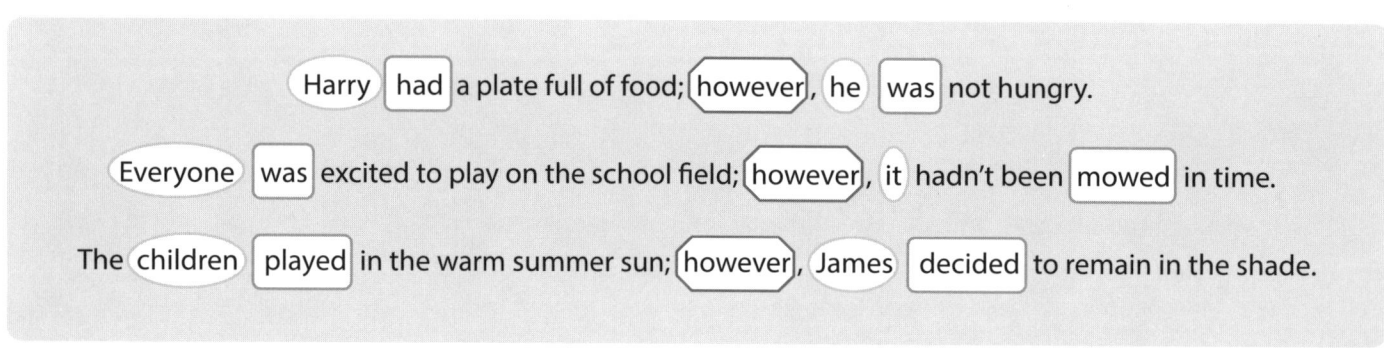

COMPLEX SENTENCES

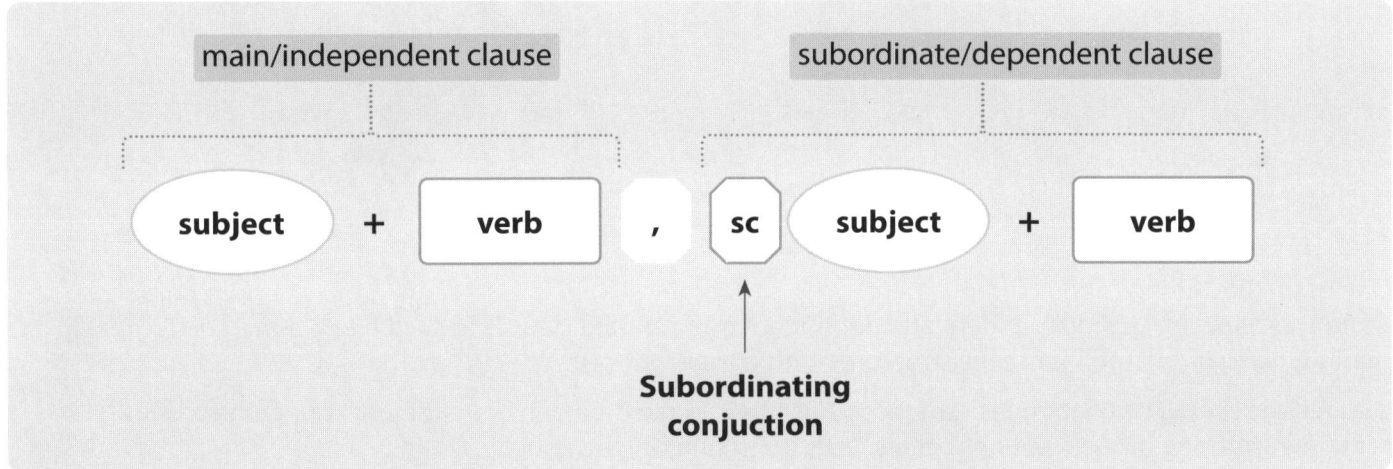

Complex sentences! Here we are. The beauty of complex sentences is that they aren't really that complex. Now we understand the structure of a clause (subject and verb), we can easily interpret the makeup of a complex sentence and how it functions.

If we look at the illustration above, we can see that a typical complex sentence has a very similar structure to a compound sentence. We have two clauses (two sets of subject and verb) and a conjunction, but this time the conjunction is a subordinating conjunction (a word that connects an independent clause with a dependent/subordinate clause that provides extra information) and it is part of one of the clauses. In the example above, the subordinating conjunction opens the second clause.

With compound sentences, we use a conjunction to join two separate and independent clauses – clauses that are independent and could form a sentence independently if we chose to punctuate. Whereas, the clauses of the complex sentence have a slightly different relationship; in order for the second clause to function, it is **dependent** on the first clause. So, whereas a compound sentence is a sentence with two independent clauses, a complex sentence is a sentence with one independent clause and at least one dependent/subordinate clause.

Example:

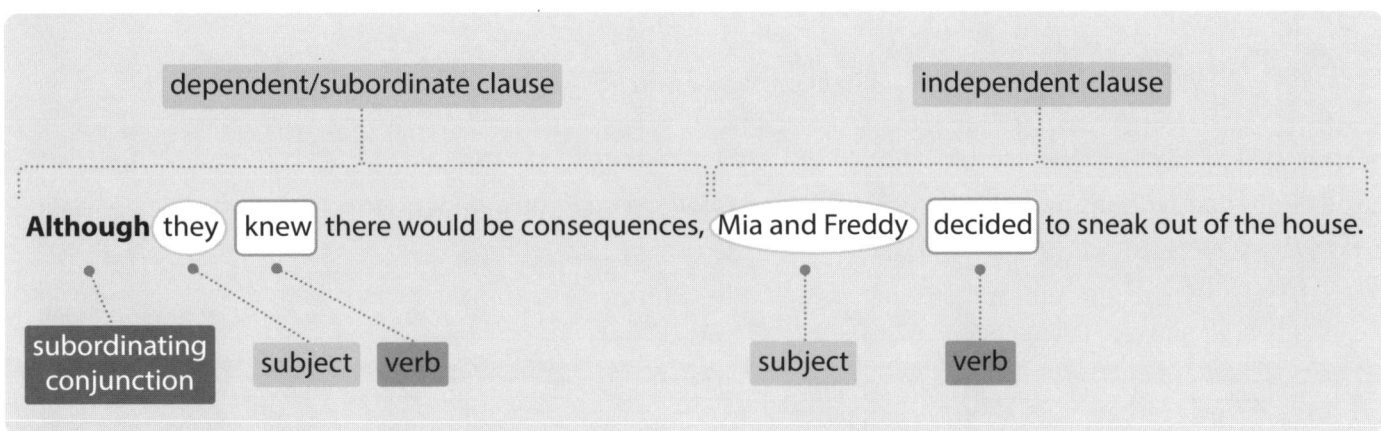

In the example above, we can see this relationship between the dependent and independent clause in a complex sentence. The subordinate/dependent clause opens with the subordinating conjunction and is dependent on the independent clause – it is unable to stand on its own.

It is possible to vary the position of the independent and subordinate/dependent clauses within the sentence – this is still a complex sentence.

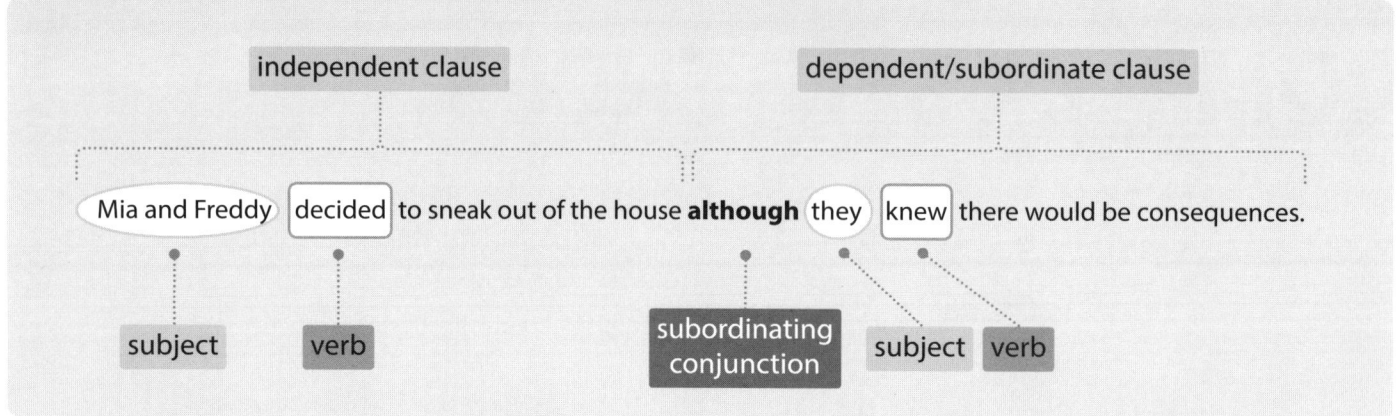

One of the best things about complex sentences is that they are flexible. As seen in the example, complex sentences allow for the independent and dependent/subordinate clauses to switch positions. This is great for pupils when varying their sentence structures within their writing.

We love the simplicity of complex sentences, but this is also where one of the biggest punctuation and sentence structure misconceptions occurs. Let's try to simplify the issue.

PUNCTUATING COMPLEX SENTENCES

One of the biggest misconceptions when it comes to compound and complex sentences is how and when the comma is used.

Grammatically, it's quite simple. If the independent clause comes first in the sentence and the dependent/subordinate clause follows, then we **don't** require a comma.

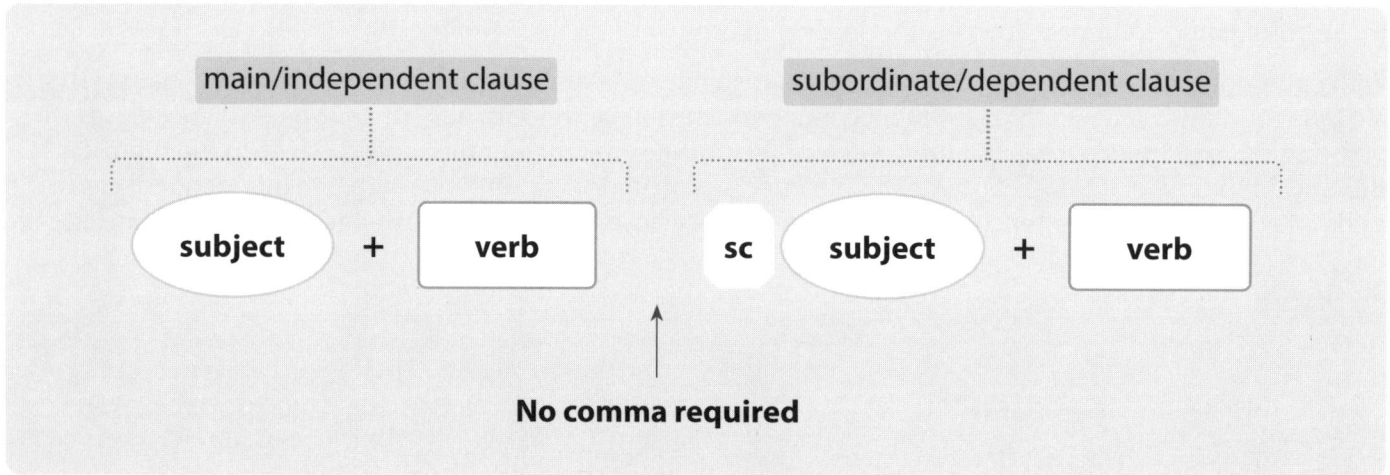

If the dependent/subordinate clause comes first and is followed by the independent clause, then we **do** require a comma.

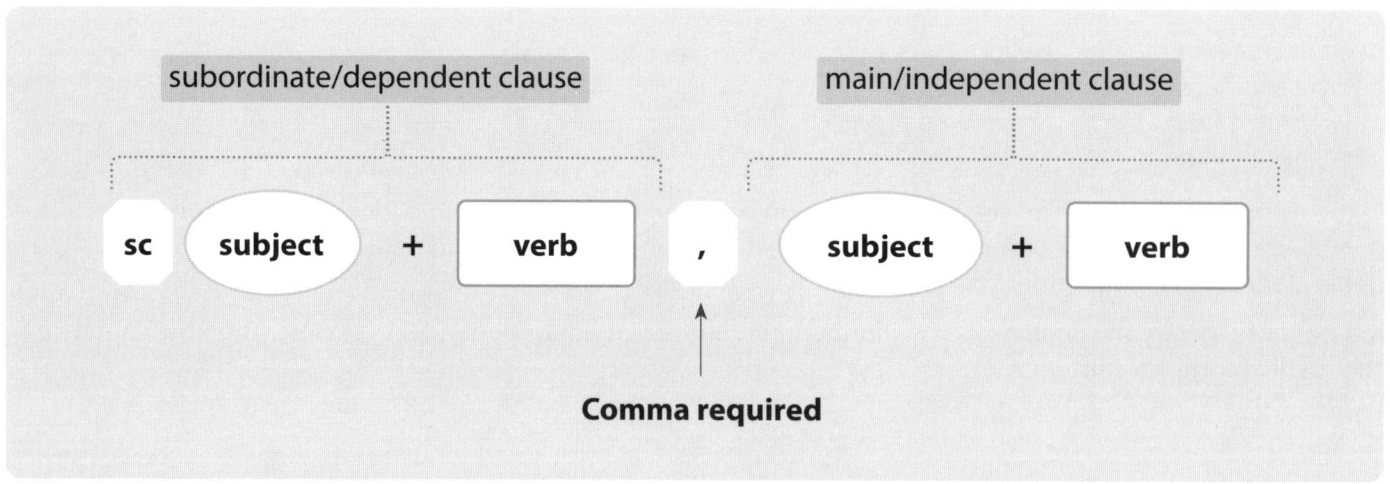

EXAMPLES OF COMPLEX SENTENCES

You can play on the field when the grass has dried.	When the grass has dried, you can play on the field.
I will come to play bingo if you bring the dabbers.	If you bring the dabbers, I will come to play bingo.
You have not finished your writing because you were not concentrating.	Because you were not concentrating, you have not finished your writing.
I want to play in the sea although I'm not sure it is safe.	Although I'm not sure it is safe, I want to play in the sea.
The puppy's legs twitched while it slept on the sofa.	While it slept on the sofa, the puppy's legs twitched.
Silvia wasn't allowed on her tablet unless she cleaned her room.	Unless she cleaned her room, Silvia wasn't allowed on her tablet.

Understanding the importance of the subject and verb can really help pupils to structure genuinely complex sentences.

EXAMPLES OF COMPLEX SENTENCES FOR SELF-ANALYSIS AND DISCUSSION

You can watch some television when you have finished your lunch.	When you have finished your lunch, you can watch some television.
I will have a sandwich if it is made with brown bread.	If it is made with brown bread, I will have a sandwich.
Courtney swam 20 lengths because she was training for a gala.	Because she was training for a gala, Courtney swam 20 lengths.
Claire wanted to book a holiday although she didn't have enough money.	Although she didn't have enough money, Claire wanted to book a holiday.
Romany drew pictures while Mum brushed her hair.	While mum brushed her hair, Romany drew pictures.
The children were not going for lunch unless their tables were tidy.	Unless their tables were tidy, the children were not going for lunch.

In a snapshot, that's the complex sentence! Not that complex after all. Now we understand the structure, we need to understand what each subordinating conjunction does. Once pupils know what each conjunction does, they will be better equipped to use them.

SUBORDINATING CONJUNCTIONS – MEANINGS AND FUNCTION

The explanations for subordinating conjunctions have been kept super simple, so that you can use these phrases consistently in school and have children use them consistently too.

WHEN

Essential Explanation: 'when' means 'at that time'.

Example 1: Frank gets nervous **when** he has to speak in public.

Example 2: **When** he has to speak in public, Frank gets nervous.

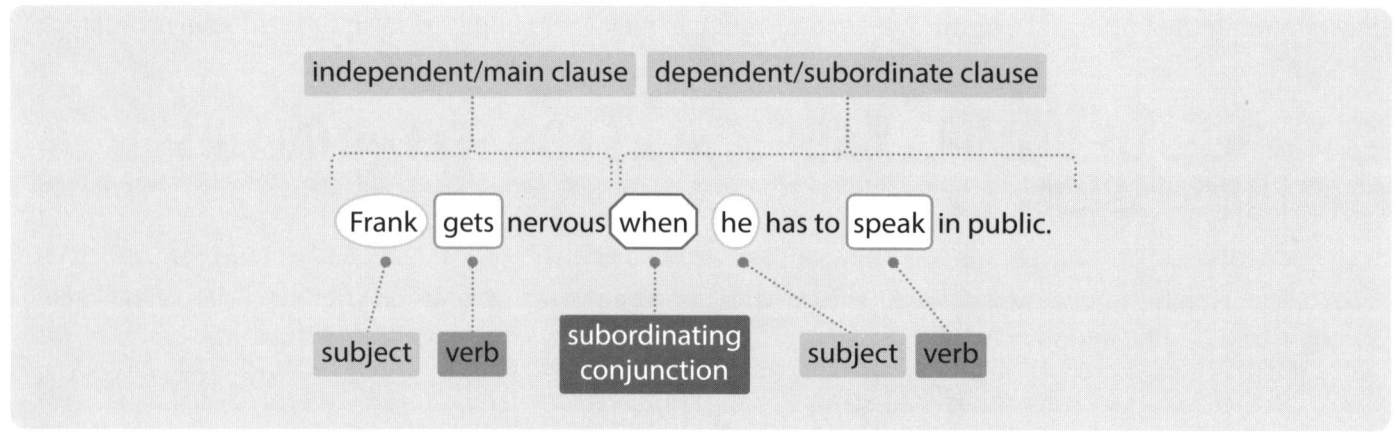

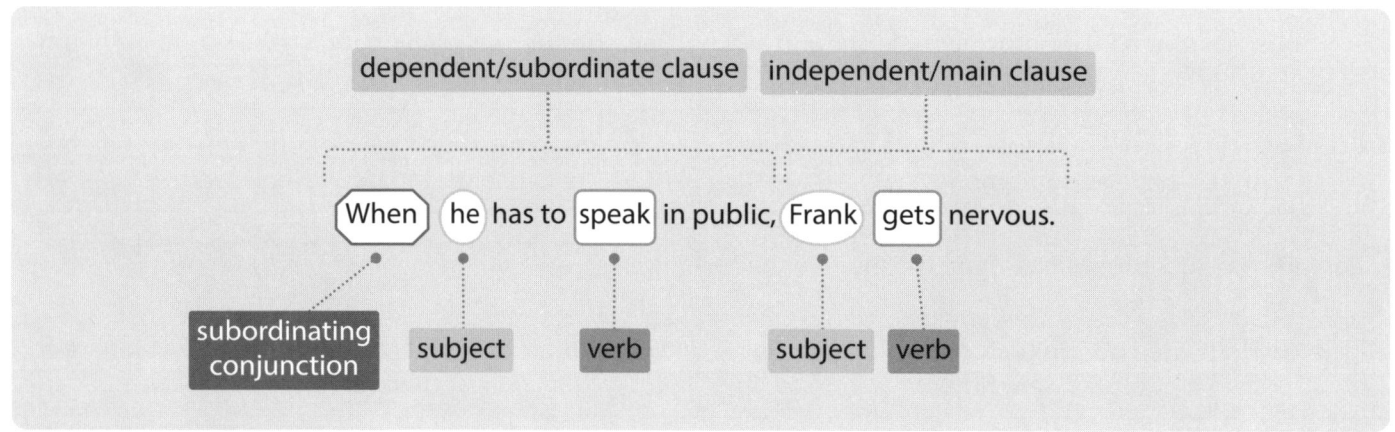

Sentence Context:

'when' is a great subordinating conjunction to start with because it is relatively simple to understand. It helps us to refer to the past, present and future. This type of sentence is also going to be useful for pupils to demonstrate their ability to vary the noun with pronouns across the two clauses. Notice in these examples how the independent clause refers to the subject as Frank, but that in the dependent clause the noun is replaced by the pronoun 'he'. Being able to avoid repetition by utilising pronouns is an important skill for pupils to be able to master.

IF

Essential Explanation: 'if' shows a condition which something else depends on.

Example 1: We can play on the grass at playtime **if** it doesn't rain.

Example 2: **If** it doesn't rain, we can play on the grass at playtime.

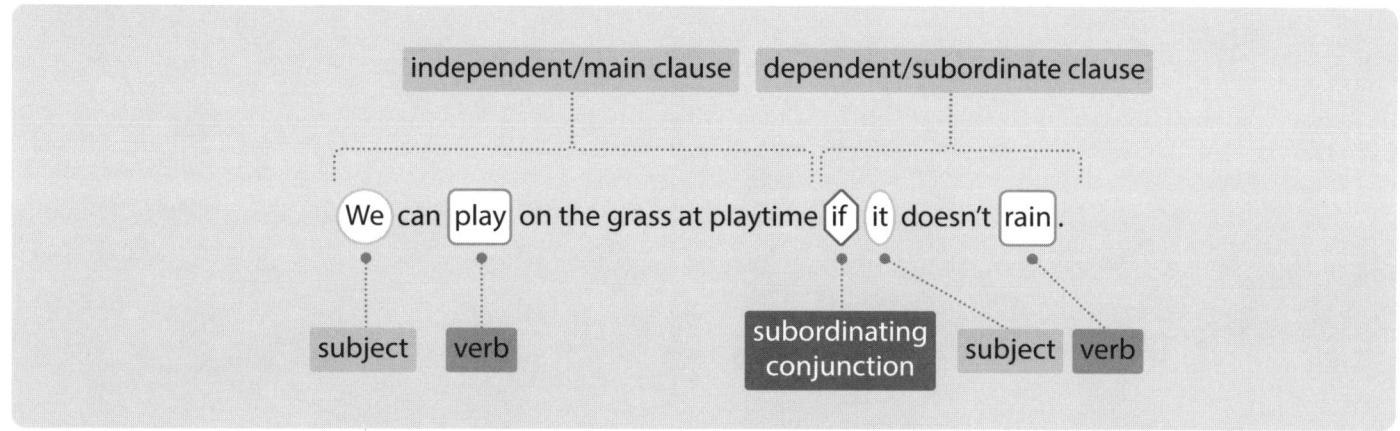

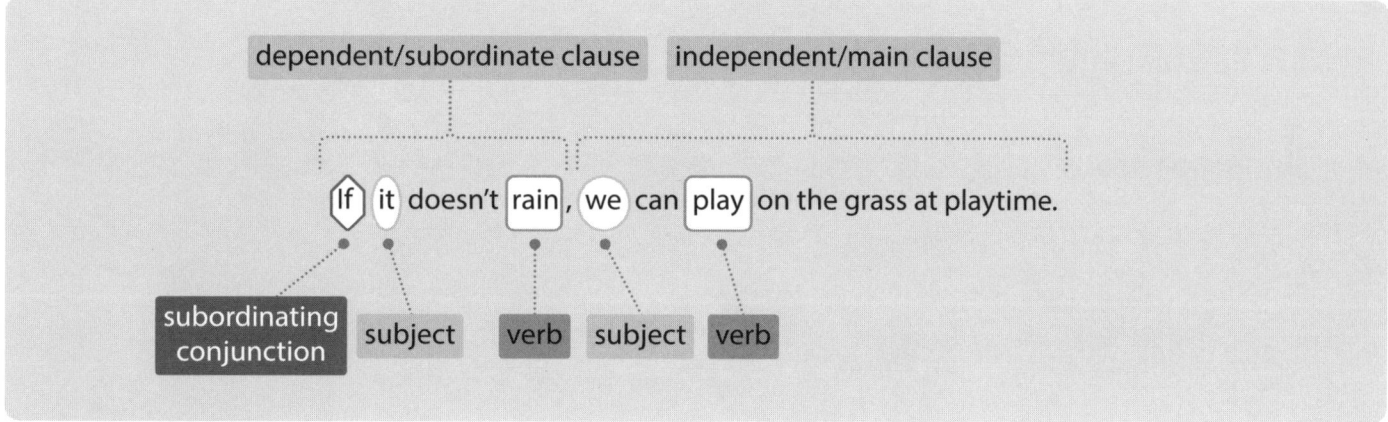

Sentence Context:

'**if**' creates something called a conditional sentence. In these sentences, the two clauses are essentially statements that state a hypothetical situation or known factor and the consequence. So, in the example, the hypothetical situation is 'we can play on the grass at playtime' and the condition is 'if it doesn't rain'. This is another great conjunction to understand, as being able to pose hypothetical and conditional situations within our writing helps to make it more complex, varied and an inferred sense of possibility. 'If' could be taught alongside 'unless', which is also conditional.

BECAUSE

Essential Explanation: 'because' explains a reason or cause.

Example 1: The football match was cancelled **because** the pitch was flooded.

Example 2: **Because** the pitch was flooded, the football match was cancelled.

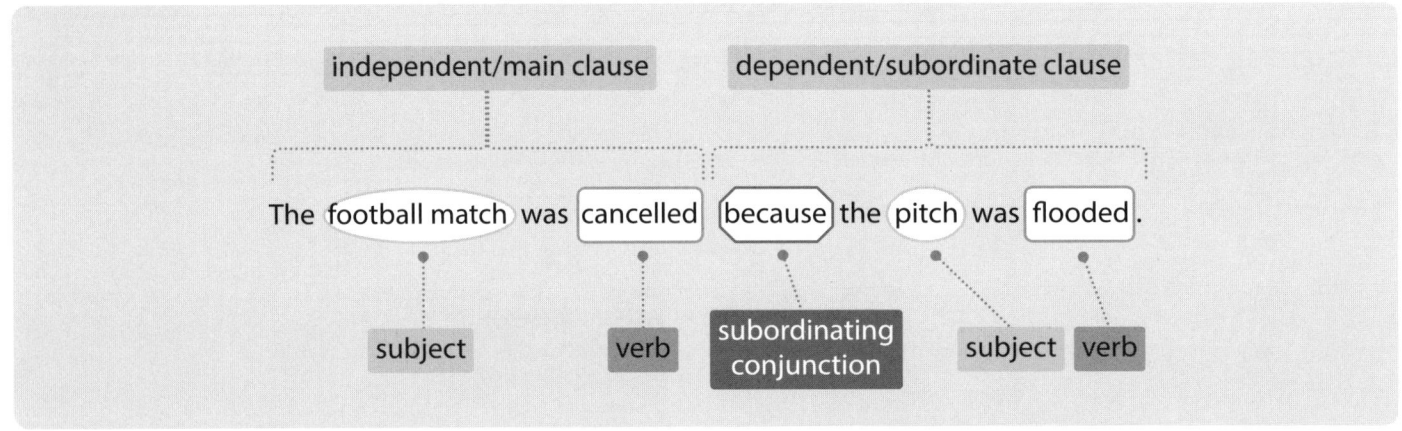

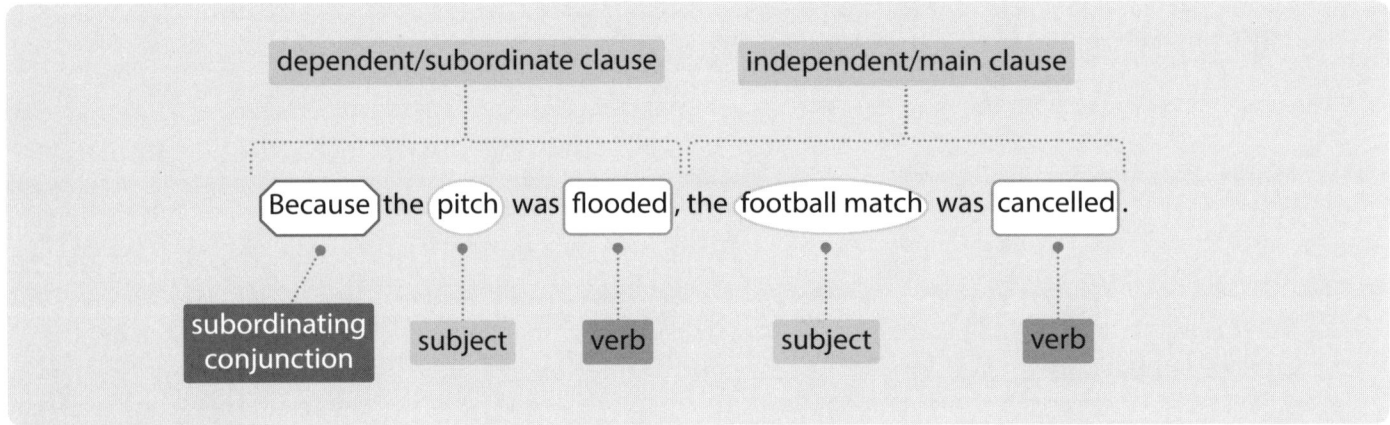

Sentence Context:

'**because**' is the quintessential subordinating conjunction, because it's commonly used within spoken language for most children. It is a classic misconception that you can't start a sentence with 'because'; however, when done in a grammatically accurate fashion – like within a complex sentence, such as Example 2 above – it's fine. In a similar way to 'and', 'because' can often be underestimated, with it being assumed that pupils know how to use 'because' with knowledge and confidence.

ALTHOUGH

Essential Explanation: 'although' connects contrasting or contradictory information.

Example 1: The girls queued for the concert tickets **although** it was raining heavily.

Example 2: **Although** it was raining heavily, the girls queued for the concert tickets.

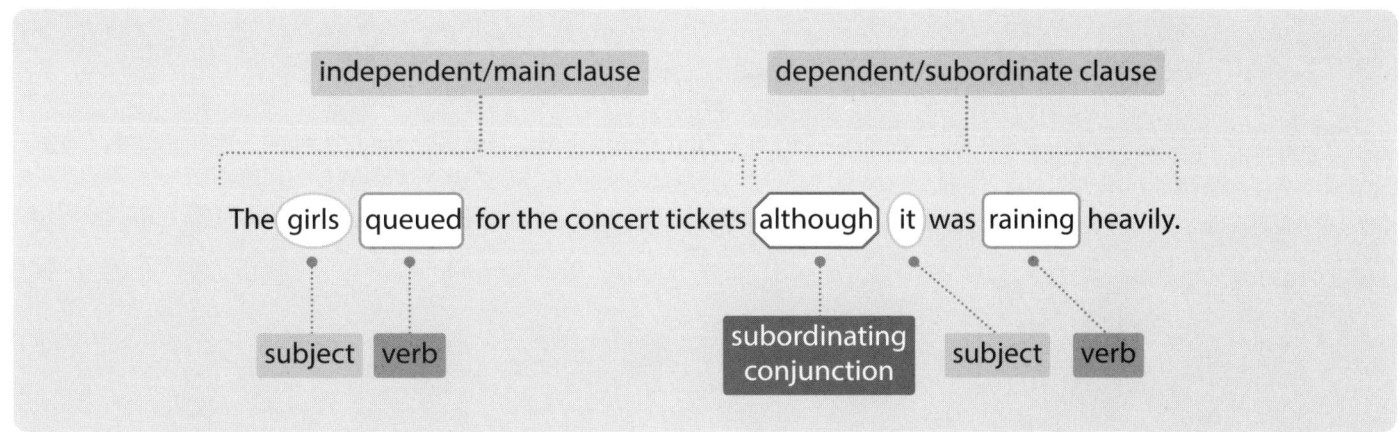

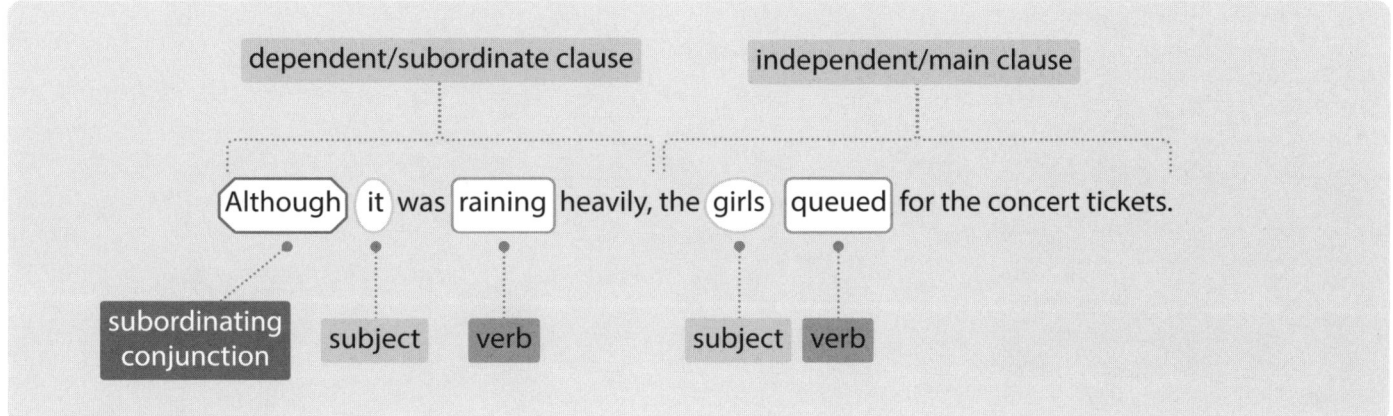

Sentence Context:

'**although**' is an amazing conjunction, due to its versatile nature and its ability to create contrast. 'Although', when used effectively, allows writers to show a contrast or something unexpected about the main clause, which might also be considered unexpected. 'Although' can also be used to show how a character or subject does something regardless of potential danger, risk or negative situation. So, in the example, although it was raining heavily, the girls queued anyway – which infers how strongly they wanted the tickets. Very simple, yet very powerful!

WHILE

Essential Explanation: 'while' shows an action or event, as another is happening.

Example 1: Mary listens to music **while** she is cooking dinner.

Example 2: **While** she is cooking dinner, Mary listens to music.

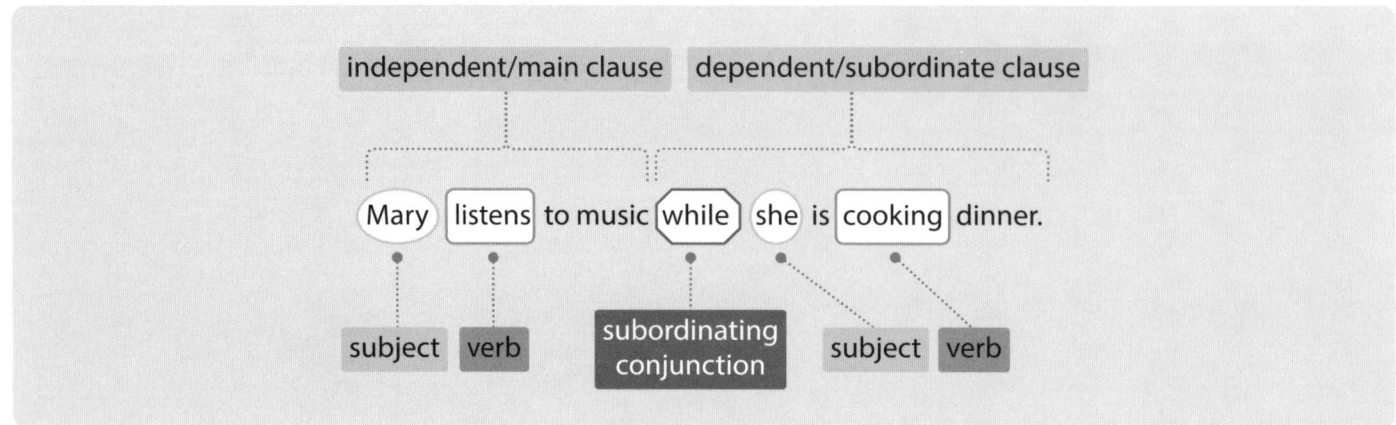

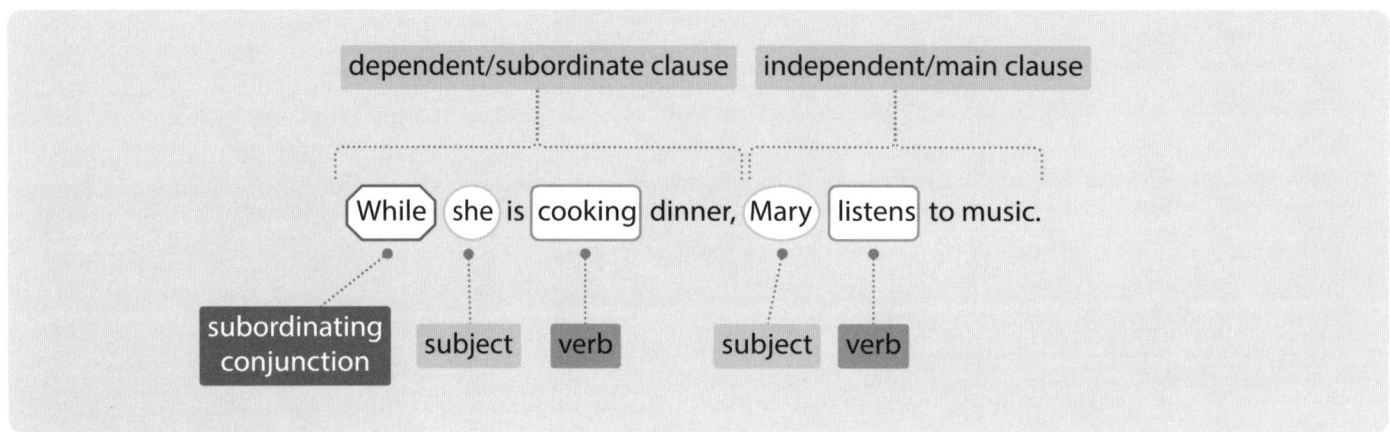

Sentence Context:

'**while**' is a really purposeful conjunction, not only because of its simplicity to understand, but also because of what it offers. 'While' enables writers to create a picture in the reader's mind of two actions being performed at the same time, which adds a serious amount of context to a character and the setting. It helps to paint a wider picture of what is going on or to convey a character's motivation. Varying the clause structure using conjunctions such as 'while' also shows intent from the author as to what action or event (of the two) the reader encounters first, and how that impacts them.

UNLESS

Essential Explanation: 'unless' shows that something will or will not happen 'unless' another action happens or a condition is met.

Example 1: I won't finish the book by Friday **unless** I read fifteen pages a day.

Example 2: **Unless** I read fifteen pages a day, I won't finish the book by Friday.

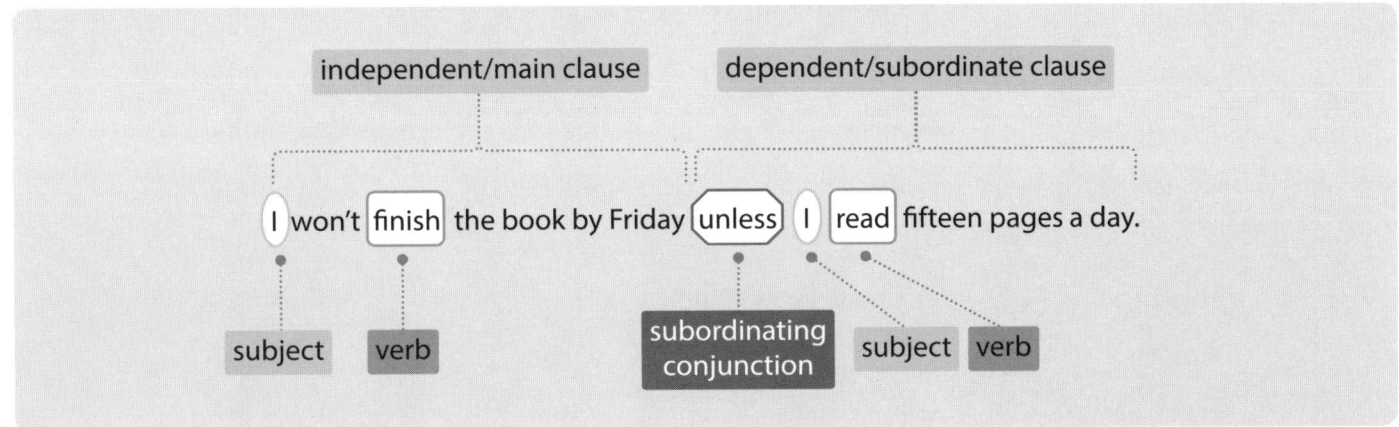

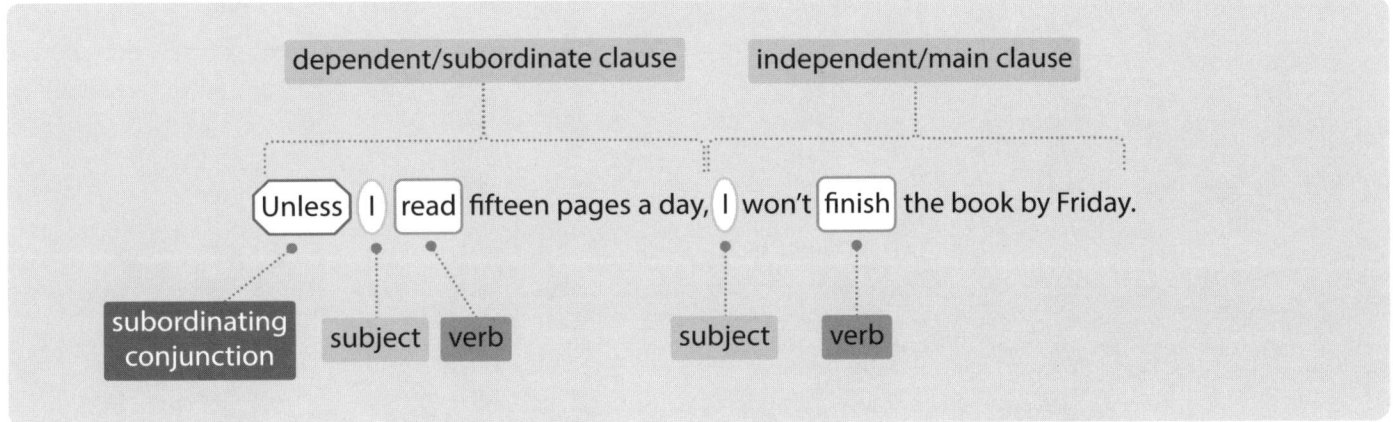

Sentence Context:

'**unless**' provides another conditional sentence structure, much like 'if'. However, whereas 'if' suggests a possibility, 'unless' is more negative, demanding and final. 'Unless' shows something will or will not happen; it's presenting a more certain outcome except if another action occurs. With practice, 'unless' can be a powerful resource in pupils' sentence-level toolkits in order to present more dramatic consequences, by varying the structure of the clause. For example:

> Unless they could find a way across the canyon, they wouldn't make it in time to save Anya.
>
> They wouldn't make it in time to save Anya unless they could find a way across the canyon.

Using 'unless' as part of the dependent/subordinate clause to open the sentence adds urgency and drama for the reader, by presenting the urgent problem first. By varying how we order the two clauses of the sentence, we are able to demonstrate our intent as an author to impact the reader. Perfect and powerful!

EVEN MORE SUBORDINATING CONJUNCTIONS

Let's remember, *Sentence Ninja* is focusing on some of the most useful and high-frequency conjunctions, but that's not to say that these are the *only* conjunctions. There are many subordinating conjunctions, each of which have a specific role within our sentences. All of these conjunctions will help to link two clauses and will open the dependent/subordinate clause, just like all of the subordinating conjunctions we have covered in the previous pages. Below is a table containing additional subordinating conjunctions, although there are many more.

SUBORDINATING CONJUNCTIONS			
after	because	lest	till
although	before	now that	unless
as	even if	provided	until
as if	even though	since	when
as long as	how	so that	whenever
as much as	if	than	where
as soon as	in as much as	that	wherever
as though	in order that	though	while

RELATIVE CLAUSES

The relative clause is one of my favourite sentence structures within the toolkit, mostly because it's really simple to master, it's extremely versatile and the punctuation associated with it is also simple to understand. Once pupils understand where and when the relative clause can occur, they can use them to add further information and vary the structure of a sentence beyond what would potentially be just a simple sentence.

The first thing to remember is our foundational understanding of what makes a clause: a subject and a verb. The relative clause acts a little bit like a subordinating conjunction in terms of structure and in that it is dependent on the clause that precedes it and cannot form a sentence on its own. This is great because if we understand the structure of the subordinate clause, the structure of the relative clause is the same. We just need to understand the relative pronoun.

In the example below, we have an independent clause that we have punctuated to create a simple sentence.

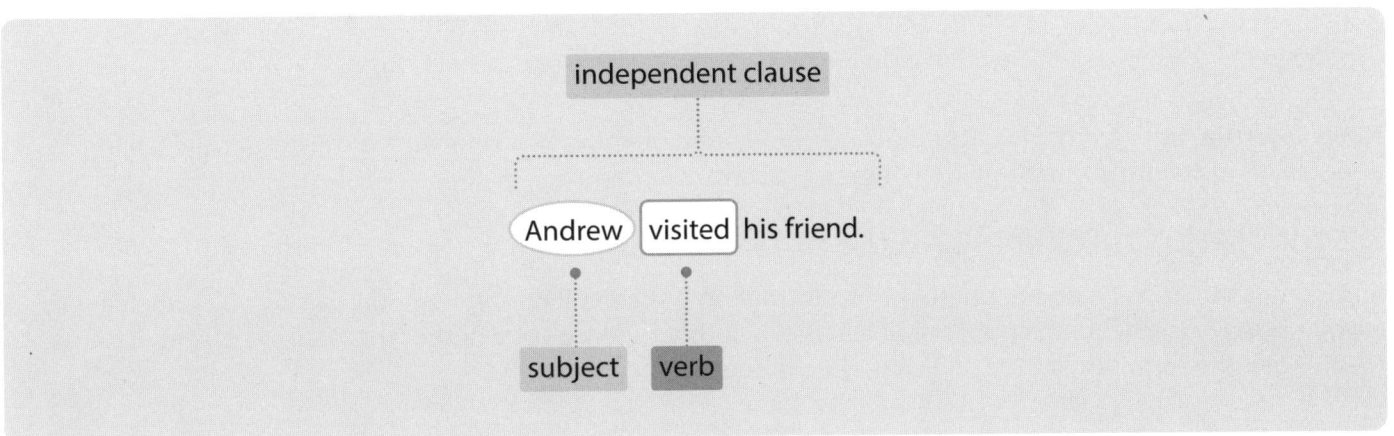

The key to being able to spot the opportunity to add a relative clause, in order to change the simple sentence to a complex sentence, is noticing that the independent clause ends in a noun or a noun phrase. In our example, the clause ends in the noun, 'friend'.

We can now use a relative clause (introduced by a relative pronoun) to link more information specifically about the friend.

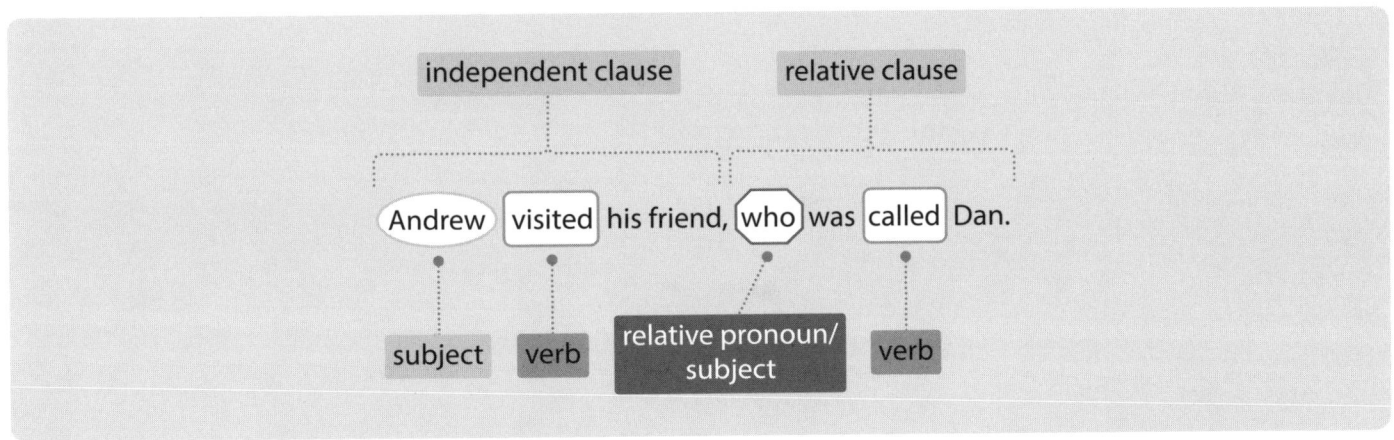

We have chosen six of the most commonly used relative pronouns for our toolkit: **who, which, that, whose, where, when**. Each is used in a slightly different situation depending on the noun or noun phrase that the previous clause ends in.

Sentence Ninja © Andrew Jennings, 2025

PUNCTUATING RELATIVE CLAUSES

ESSENTIAL RELATIVE CLAUSE

An essential relative clause provides crucial information about the noun it modifies, and so it is necessary for the sentence's meaning. In this instance, a comma **is not** used.

I like to sit in the garden **when** the sun is shining.

Jeremy watched the angry dog **which** was drooling.

NON-ESSENTIAL RELATIVE CLAUSE

A non-essential relative clause provides additional information that is not essential to the meaning of the sentence. In this instance, a comma **is** used.

They went to the beach, **where** they had space to run and play.

The team won the competition, **which** was very exciting.

Note: **Essential** (no comma) really helps us to understand or know *who* or *what* we are specifically talking about; if it's just extra information then it's **non-essential** (comma).

MISCONCEPTIONS REGARDING THE USE OF THE COMMA

Sometimes the decision about whether the information is essential or non-essential can be quite unclear or ambiguous. Try to encourage pupils to at least consciously think about whether the clause is essential to the meaning of the sentence; if they think it is, then it doesn't need a comma.

RELATIVE EMBEDDED CLAUSE

The relative embedded clause is a simple continuation of the relative clause; the only difference is that the relative embedded clause is 'embedded' within the sentence. Let's take a look.

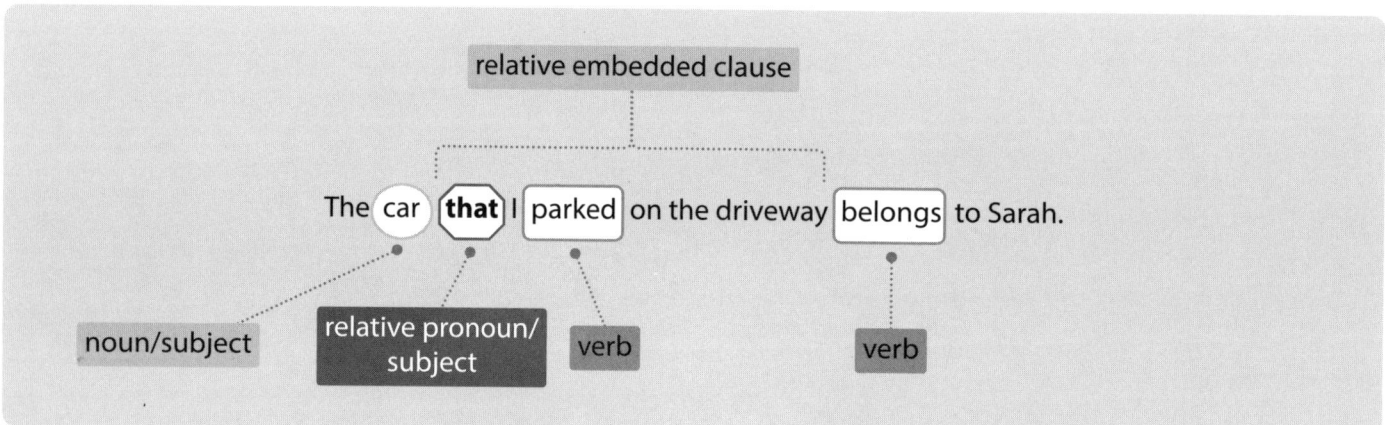

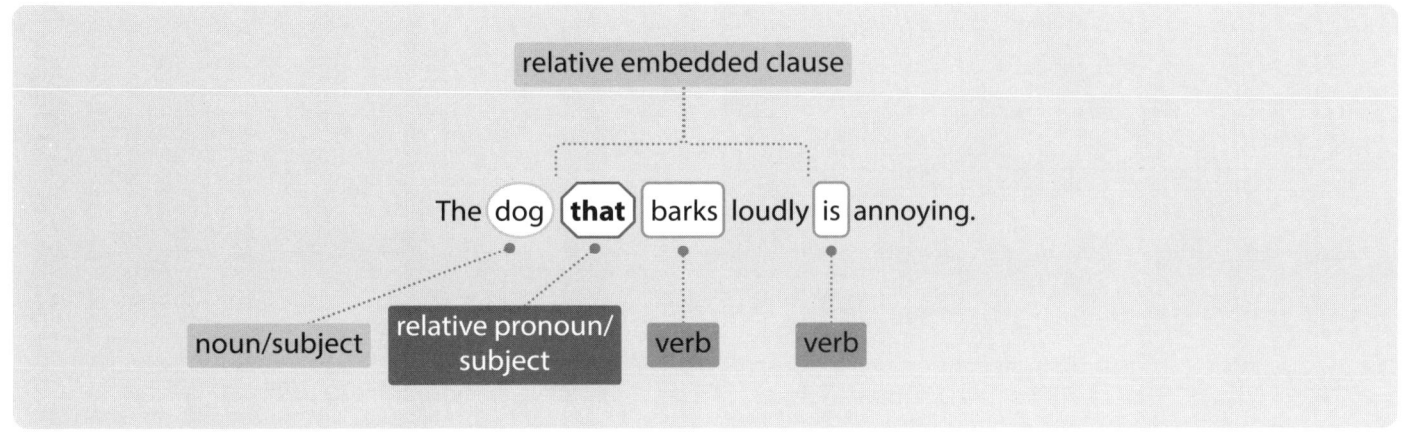

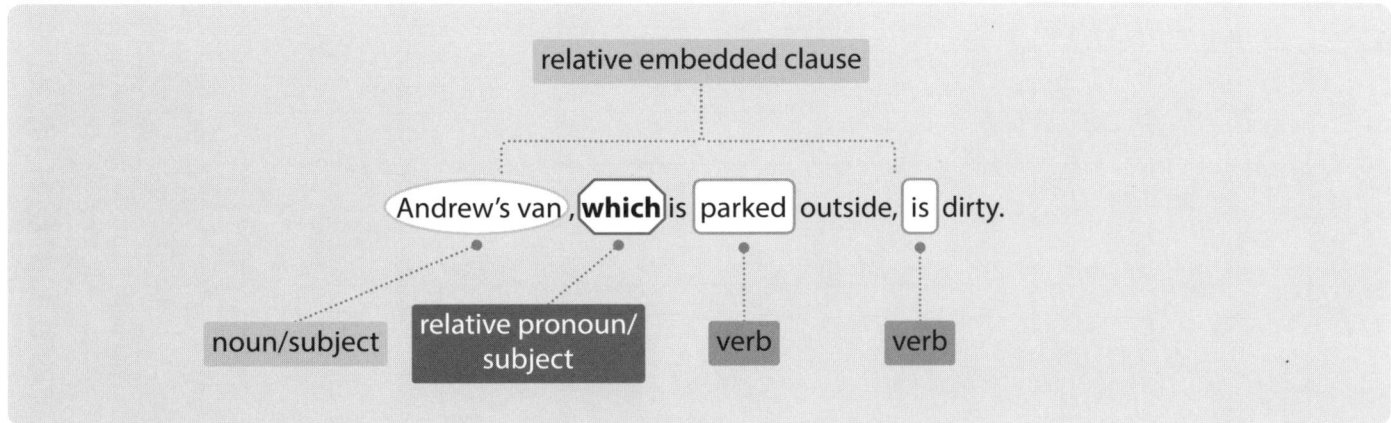

In all of the examples above, we have a clause embedded within another. The embedded clause develops from the noun or noun phrase, adding more information about the noun or noun phrase.

The way of knowing that we have a well-structured embedded relative clause is, if we removed it, we would still have an independent clause that could function as a sentence on its own. This is true of all the examples above.

PUNCTUATING RELATIVE EMBEDDED CLAUSES

The same rules apply as they did for punctuating relative clauses. If the embedded clause is **essential** then the clause does *not* need punctuating with commas. If the relative clause is **non-essential**, then we *would* use two commas to show where the clause starts and finishes. It's that simple.

Again, the ideal approach is for pupils to think about and make the best punctuation decisions they can. Encourage them to see how their sentences read with and without the commas and to go with their gut if they are not sure. The great thing about relative embedded clauses is that the sentence should still read well regardless.

SENTENCE COMPETENCE CHECKLIST (ESSENTIAL SENTENCE TOOLKIT)

Name	Clause		Sentence	Compound Sentence – Coordinating Conjunction						Conjunctive Adverb	Complex Sentence – Subordinating Conjunction					Relative Clause – Relative Pronoun					Embedded Relative Clause	
	subject	verb	simple	and	but	so	yet	or	for	nor	however	when	if	because	although	while	unless	who	which	that	whose	where	when	RP

Sentence Ninja © Andrew Jennings, 2025

PART 4
ESSENTIAL SENTENCE NINJA TOOLKIT: PRACTICE

SIMPLE SENTENCES (SUBJECT + VERB)

EXPLICIT MODELLING EXAMPLES AND ACTIVITIES

These examples are purely for teachers and pupils to discuss and explore. Teachers could type these simple sentences on the whiteboard in order to model to pupils how to create a simple sentence with a subject and a verb. Pupils can actively identify the subject and the verb by circling the subject and drawing a rectangle around the verb. This can be discussed as part of the modelling.

The (family) [spent] the day in the garden.	The (puppy) [chewed] on the bone.
(Paul) [played] outside.	Three (birds) [landed] on the fence.
The (clouds) [filled] the sky.	(Mum) [took] the chicken out of the oven.
(Alex) [asked] a question.	The (car) [zoomed] along the street.
Our (wellies) [squelched] in the mud.	(Liam) [painted] a lovely picture.
The (wind) [snapped] the branch.	The (sea) [battered] the beach.
The (phone) [rang].	(Alex) [dug] a deep hole.
Lots of (people) [visit] London.	The (friends) [shared] the popcorn.
(Sammy) [fell] to the ground.	The (chocolate) [melted] in the sun.
The (plant) [grew] in the warm sun.	The (bus) [stopped] every minute.

DICTATION SENTENCE ACTIVITIES

Sentence-level dictation is an important aspect of low-pressure sentence-level exposure. Teachers should dictate the sentences to the pupils, making it clear that the objective is to write a simple sentence, containing a subject and a verb. When each sentence has been written down by the pupils, they should indicate the subject by drawing a circle around it and the verb by drawing a rectangle around it, before discussing with the teacher what the subject and verb might be and why.

Dictating two sentences a day provides great exposure to the composition of sentences, and is an opportunity for discussion and clarity for pupils. Alternatively, the 20 examples below can be used at teachers' discretion to provide dictation opportunities for simple sentences.

M	The (fish) [swam] in the sea.	An (eagle) [swooped] from the sky.
T	(Alex) [wished] for a bike.	(I) [want] some chocolate.
W	(Jenny) [danced] at the disco.	(We) [called] for our friend.
T	The (group) all [played] the game.	An (ant) [carried] a leaf.
F	(Fred) [hoped] to win.	Two (boys) [chased] each other.
M	(I) [read] my book in the sun.	My (sister) [gave] me a nice present.
T	(She) [twisted] the dirty cloth.	(We) [cleaned] our smelly bin.
W	The (dog) [chased] the ball.	The (girls) [visited] the bowling alley.
T	(Paul) [ate] his jam roll and crisps.	The (witch) [cast] a wicked spell.
F	(Lights) [flashed] on the car.	(He) [ripped] his top.

COMPLETE THE SENTENCE

These activities require pupils to complete the sentence by adding additional words. The words they add will need to include a verb. Pupils should be encouraged to punctuate the clause with a full stop to form a complete sentence. Pupils should also circle the subject and draw a rectangle around the verb. This can be discussed when the sentences are shared.

Complete and punctuate the clause to make a simple sentence.

(Example) The girls <u>messaged each other on their phones.</u>

Our car _____

The friends _____

Paul _____

A lorry _____

Complete and punctuate the clause to make a simple sentence.

The lion _____

My sister _____

The spaceship _____

The knight _____

An eagle _____

Complete and punctuate the clause to make a simple sentence.

Julia _____

My teacher _____

Auntie Meg _____

Courtney and Mia _____

The team _____

Sentence Ninja © Andrew Jennings, 2025

MISSING WORD SENTENCES

In the missing word activities, pupils are given incomplete sentences to complete. There will be many words that can be added to complete the sentences so that they make sense. Some sentences will already contain a subject or verb, so pupils will need to think about what is required. Pupils should circle the subjects and draw rectangles around the verbs. When the pupils have completed the tasks, what they have written can be discussed.

Complete the sentences by adding a subject, verb or both.

(Example) The <u>fish</u> powerfully <u>jumped</u> out of the water.

My _____ was _____ from our shed.

_____ built a huge sandcastle.

A purple _____ spread its feathers.

Robert slowly _____ up the mountain.

Complete the sentences by adding a subject, verb or both.

Hugh _____ many miles.

Julia _____ a delicious meal for her family.

Unfortunately, Arjan _____ his arm.

The _____ slowly _____ up the tree.

Jamila _____ a large hat in the sun.

Complete the sentences by adding a subject, verb or both.

Our _____ has great teachers.

The _____ loudly _____ in the distance.

Ruby _____ the song in front of everyone.

Kamal _____ the letter through the letterbox.

_____ rushed to the front of the queue.

WORD JUMBLE

Word jumbles have all the required words to form a sentence, but unfortunately they are jumbled up! Pupils need to unjumble and rewrite the sentence. Encouraging pupils to identify possible subjects and verbs can help to create a logical order. Ask the pupils to punctuate each sentence correctly when they have unjumbled them.

Unjumble the words and rewrite the sentences in the spaces below. Remember to punctuate the sentences.

killer whale   seal   the   chased   the

_____

are   birthday   my   for   visiting   my   friends

_____

Unjumble the words and rewrite the sentences in the spaces below. Remember to punctuate the sentences.

the   read   Mr Robson   class   to   book   the

_____

warmed   the   sun   face   my

_____

Unjumble the words and rewrite the sentences in the spaces below. Remember to punctuate the sentences.

the   the   over   ball   kicked   Alex   fence

_____

is   beach   the   to   walking   my   sister

_____

Sentence Ninja © Andrew Jennings, 2025

COMPOUND SENTENCES (COORDINATING CONJUNCTION)

A note on modal and auxiliary verbs

As sentences become more advanced, they will contain modal verbs (verbs indicating possibility or necessity, such as 'could' and 'should'), and auxiliary verbs (helping verbs, such as 'was' and 'had'), which help the main verb within the sentence to function. For the purposes of this book, we are focusing solely on the main verb.

EXPLICIT MODELLING EXAMPLES AND ACTIVITIES

These examples are for teachers and pupils to discuss and explore. Teachers could type these simple sentences on the whiteboard to model to pupils how to create a simple sentence with a subject and at least one verb. Pupils can identify the subjects and verbs by circling the subjects and drawing rectangles around the verbs. This can be discussed as part of the modelling. As the teacher types or writes, it is vital to continuously reference clauses as they are created, as well as the conjunctions joining them.

As part of the modelling exercise, remember to explain and reinforce what each conjunction is doing and its function in the sentence. See the section on compound sentences for more information (page 38).

My (dog) [played] with the ball, **and** the (cat) [lay] in the sun.
(Alice) [cleaned] her room, **and** (she) [took] out the rubbish.
The (sun) [rose] from below the horizon, **and** the (birds) [sang].

(Bickers United) [lost] the final, **but** the (players) [tried] their best.
(I) [wanted to read], **but** (we) [visited] my auntie instead.
(Rain) [fell] from the sky, **but** the (sun) soon [dried] the playground.

(Jeremy) [put] the fruit in the fridge, **so** (he) could [eat] it later.
(Dad) [cut] the grass, **so** the (kids) could [play] football.
(School) [finished] early today, **so** the (choir) could [sing] on the playground.

(Aisha) [bought] a phone for her birthday, **yet** (she) [lost] it the next day.
The (school field) [was] dry, **yet** (no one) [played] on it.
(Annie) [knew] the answer, **yet** (she) [kept] it to herself.

Should (Robert) [eat] cornflakes, **or** should (he) [have] wheat hoops?
(They) could [climb] up the cliff, **or** (they) could [tunnel] under the rocks.
(Maggie) [wondered] if she should chop the fruit in half, **or** if (she) should [slice] it thinly.

(Andrew) didn't [know] his times tables, **nor** did (he) [know] his division facts.
(Mia) [was] not very friendly, **nor** [was] (she) kind.
(Faye) hadn't [remembered] her coat, **nor** had (she) [brought] her lunch.

(Laticia) [closed] the door, **for** a (draught) [made] her cold.
(Mrs Smith) [read] the story out loud, **for** (everyone) [requested] that she do so.
The foul (beast) [waited] outside, **for** the (knight) [challenged] it to a duel.

Once comfortable with the routine and structure of explicit modelling, teachers can create their own sentences to model.

DICTATION SENTENCE ACTIVITIES

Sentence-level dictation is an important aspect of low-pressure sentence-level exposure. Teachers should dictate the sentences to the pupils, making it clear that the objective is to write a compound sentence containing two clauses, each with a subject, and at least one verb and the correct punctuation. When each sentence has been written down by the pupils, they should indicate the subject by circling it and the verb by drawing a rectangle around it, before discussing with the teacher what the subject and verb might be and why.

The huge (dragon) [landed] in the field, **and** (it) [breathed] fire across the land.
(Bella) [fought] to the front of the queue, **but** all of the (tickets) [sold] out.
(Remi) [spoke] to Mr Kim, **so** (he) could [say] sorry for his actions.
(Aliens) [landed] on the playground, **yet** the (children) [weren't] interested.
(Sal) [wondered] if it was time for a snack, **or** did (she) need to [wait] until lunch?
(He) didn't [like] to run, **nor** did (he) [enjoy] swimming.
The (farmer) [covered] the straw, **for** a (storm) [approached].

The (bread) [was] warm, **and** the (butter) [melted].
(She) [was] right, **but** (she) [kept] quiet.
(Robbie) [finished] his homework quickly, **so** (he) could [play] outside.
(He) had [eaten] far too much, **yet** (he) couldn't [stop] eating.
(You) can [have] ice cream for dessert, **or** (you) can [have] a biscuit.
(John) could neither [find] his keys, **nor** could (he) [remember] where he left them.
(He) [gave up] his dreams, **for** (he) [loved] her dearly.

COMPLETE THE SENTENCE

These activities require pupils to complete the sentence by adding the additional clause. The words they add will need to include a subject and a verb. Pupils should be encouraged to punctuate the second clause with a full stop to form a complete, compound sentence. Pupils should also circle the subject and draw a rectangle around the main verb in each sentence. This can be discussed when the completed sentences are shared.

Complete and punctuate the clause to make a compound sentence. When you have done this, circle the subject and draw a rectangle around the verb.

Mia sliced the bread, **and** _____

Mia sliced the bread, **but** _____

Mia sliced the bread, **so** _____

Complete and punctuate the clause to make a compound sentence. When you have done this, circle the subject and draw a rectangle around the verb.

My dog barked loudly, **and** _____

My dog barked loudly, **but** _____

My dog barked loudly, **so** _____

Complete and punctuate the clause to make a compound sentence. When you have done this, circle the subject and draw a rectangle around the verb.

I felt too tired to get out of bed, **and** _____

I felt too tired to get out of bed, **but** _____

I felt too tired to get out of bed, **so** _____

Complete and punctuate the clause to make a compound sentence. When you have done this, circle the subject and draw a rectangle around the verb.

The wolf sniffed the cold air, **and** _____

The wolf sniffed the cold air, **but** _____

The wolf sniffed the cold air, **so** _____

Complete and punctuate the clause to make a compound sentence. When you have done this, circle the subject and draw a rectangle around the verb.

Trees waved in the autumn wind, **and** _____

Trees waved in the autumn wind, **but** _____

Trees waved in the autumn wind, **so** _____

Complete and punctuate the clause to make a compound sentence. When you have done this, circle the subject and draw a rectangle around the verb.

The witch stirred the soup in the cauldron, **and** _____

The witch stirred the soup in the cauldron, **but** _____

The witch stirred the soup in the cauldron, **so** _____

Sentence Ninja © Andrew Jennings, 2025

COMPLETE THE SENTENCE

Complete and punctuate the clause to make a compound sentence. When you have done this, circle the subject and draw a rectangle around the verb.

John paid for the food with a £5 note, **and** _____

John paid for the food with a £5 note, **but** _____

John paid for the food with a £5 note, **so** _____

John paid for the food with a £5 note, **yet** _____

Complete and punctuate the clause to make a compound sentence. When you have done this, circle the subject and draw a rectangle around the verb.

Alice screamed for help, **and** _____

Alice screamed for help, **but** _____

Alice screamed for help, **so** _____

Alice screamed for help, **yet** _____

Complete and punctuate the clause to make a compound sentence. When you have done this, circle the subject and draw a rectangle around the verb.

The erupting volcano spat lava into the air, **and** _____

The erupting volcano spat lava into the air, **but** _____

The erupting volcano spat lava into the air, **so** _____

The erupting volcano spat lava into the air, **yet** _____

Complete and punctuate the clause to make a compound sentence. When you have done this, circle the subject and draw a rectangle around the verb.

Before the game, Fred took a huge, deep breath, **and** _____

Before the game, Fred took a huge, deep breath, **but** _____

Before the game, Fred took a huge, deep breath, **so** _____

Before the game, Fred took a huge, deep breath, **yet** _____

Complete and punctuate the clause to make a compound sentence. When you have done this, circle the subject and draw a rectangle around the verb.

Mrs Jones took Class 5 for a walk on the beach, **and** _____

Mrs Jones took Class 5 for a walk on the beach, **but** _____

Mrs Jones took Class 5 for a walk on the beach, **so** _____

Mrs Jones took Class 5 for a walk on the beach, **yet** _____

COMPLETE THE SENTENCE

Complete and punctuate the clause to make a compound sentence. When you have done this, circle the subject and draw a rectangle around the verb.

Mia sliced the bread, **yet** _____

The jar was filled right to the top with water, **yet** _____

The war was finally over, **yet** _____

Complete and punctuate the clause to make a compound sentence. When you have done this, circle the subject and draw a rectangle around the verb.

You can go to the park, **or** _____

Was it going to rain, **or** _____

Would the dragon destroy the city, **or** _____

Complete and punctuate the clause to make a compound sentence. When you have done this, circle the subject and draw a rectangle around the verb.

He neither had the energy to get up, **nor** _____

The dog didn't want to fetch the ball, **nor** _____

The classroom was not hot, **nor** _____

Complete and punctuate the clause to make a compound sentence. When you have done this, circle the subject and draw a rectangle around the verb.

Mr Halfpenny wore his best clothes to the ball, **for** _____

He wrote the last letter he might ever write, **for** _____

They shivered, covered in snow and ice, **for** _____

Sentence Ninja © Andrew Jennings, 2025

COMPLETE THE SENTENCE – 'HOWEVER'

The first resource includes the punctuation associated with 'however' as a scaffold.

Complete and punctuate the clause with 'however' to make a compound sentence. When you have done this, circle the subject and draw a rectangle around the verb.
Tia decided to visit the dark woods; **however,** _____
The sprint event was about to begin; **however,** _____
Alfie had forgotten his great idea; **however,** _____
Mark and Asif wanted to have a sleepover; **however,** _____

The second resource encourages pupils to add the semicolon and comma punctuation independently.

Complete and punctuate the clause with 'however' to make a compound sentence. When you have done this, circle the subject and draw a rectangle around the verb.
They had reached the temple on the map _____
My family was going on holiday _____
The boat began to sink in the ocean _____
Earthquakes can be very dangerous _____

CLAUSE COMBINING

Below are 8 independent clauses. Use the conjunctions to join the clauses and write out 4 complete sentences. Each conjunction should only be used once. Remember to punctuate the sentences.

and	but	so	yet
Rob put the cutlery on the table		the children sat inside watching television	
the sun was warm and relaxing		mum decided to cut the lawn	
Alice wanted to play in the garden		he forgot the table mats	
the grass was long and full of weeds		she wanted to fill up the paddling pool	

Below are 8 independent clauses. Use the conjunctions to join the clauses and write out 4 complete sentences. Each conjunction should only be used once. Remember to punctuate the sentences.

and	but	so	yet
mum was visiting her friend		she could impress her friends	
the argument was over		he decided to walk anyway	
Jen learned a new dance move		Marco was still angry	
he had enough money to get the bus		dad was painting the shed	

Below are 8 independent clauses. Use the conjunctions to join the clauses and write out 4 complete sentences. Each conjunction should only be used once. Remember to punctuate the sentences.

and	but	so	yet
Arlo sang as loud as he could		he would go on to do it again	
the bear devoured the fish		the mashed potato was so soft	
he made a huge mistake		it was still hungry for more	
the gravy was very hot		his parents could hear him	

Below are 8 independent clauses. Use the conjunctions to join the clauses and write out 4 complete sentences. Each conjunction should only be used once. Remember to punctuate the sentences.

and	but	so	yet
the ants collected the leaves		she was scared to go inside	
she stood outside the door		she cleaned her teeth	
Kevin needed to draw a straight line		they could feed the colony	
Scarlet brushed her hair		he didn't have a ruler	

PRINTABLE PROMPTS

Print, cut and stick these sentence challenges into your pupils' books. Encourage pupils to create specific compound sentences and to think about the role the conjunction plays in the sentence, as well as the presence of the subject and the main verb in each clause.

'and' – Sentence Challenge

Write three separate sentences using '**and**' as the coordinating conjunction.

Remember that '**and**' **joins two clauses**. Each clause should contain a subject and a verb.

When you have finished each sentence, underline the conjunction, circle the subject and draw a rectangle around the verb in each clause.

'yet' – Sentence Challenge

Write three separate sentences using '**yet**' as the coordinating conjunction.

Remember that '**yet**' **contrasts two clauses** (like 'but'). Each clause should contain a subject and a verb.

When you have finished each sentence, underline the conjunction, circle the subject and draw a rectangle around the verb in each clause.

'but' – Sentence Challenge

Write three separate sentences using '**but**' as the coordinating conjunction.

Remember that '**but**' **contrasts two clauses**. Each clause should contain a subject and a verb.

When you have finished each sentence, underline the conjunction, circle the subject and draw a rectangle around the verb in each clause.

'or' – Sentence Challenge

Write three separate sentences using '**or**' as the coordinating conjunction.

Remember that '**or**' **joins two clauses to show two options, alternatives or possibilities**. Each clause should contain a subject and a verb.

When you have finished each sentence, underline the conjunction, circle the subject and draw a rectangle around the verb in each clause.

'so' – Sentence Challenge

Write three separate sentences using '**so**' as the coordinating conjunction.

Remember that '**so**' **is used to show the result or the 'why?' of the first clause**. Each clause should contain a subject and a verb.

When you have finished each sentence, underline the conjunction, circle the subject and draw a rectangle around the verb in each clause.

'nor' or 'for' – Sentence Challenge

Write three separate sentences using '**nor**' or '**for**' as the coordinating conjunction.

Remember that '**nor**' **joins two negative clauses** and '**for**' **explains why** (like 'because'). Each clause should contain a subject and a verb.

When you have finished each sentence, underline the conjunction, circle the subject and draw a rectangle around the verb in each clause.

FORMATIVE ASSESSMENT PROMPTS

The resources found on the following pages can be used within a classroom or across the whole school to assess and track pupils' sentence-level skill. The prompts are relatively simple prompts, which ask pupils to write specific sentence types that require the pupils to demonstrate their ability to create those particular sentence types.

These can be completed easily and within a short time period of around five minutes. It is advisable to make this assessment extremely informal, to the point where the pupils see it as just another task, rather than an assessment. The information gleaned from the assessments will help teachers to better understand and track the depth and wealth of each pupil's sentence-level toolkit.

Sentence Toolkit Task
Compound Sentence – 'and'

Task: You must write two compound sentences using the conjunction '**and**'.

Leave a line between each sentence. Each sentence must be punctuated correctly.

Tip: Remember to think about the subject and the verb.

Tip: If you are struggling for inspiration, think about a setting, character or situation from a book you are reading.

Sentence Toolkit Task
Compound Sentence – 'yet'

Task: You must write two compound sentences using the conjunction '**yet**'.

Leave a line between each sentence. Each sentence must be punctuated correctly.

Tip: Remember to think about the subject and the verb.

Tip: If you are struggling for inspiration, think about a setting, character or situation from a book you are reading.

Sentence Toolkit Task
Compound Sentence – 'but'

Task: You must write two compound sentences using the conjunction '**but**'.

Leave a line between each sentence. Each sentence must be punctuated correctly.

Tip: Remember to think about the subject and the verb.

Tip: If you are struggling for inspiration, think about a setting, character or situation from a book you are reading.

Sentence Toolkit Task
Compound Sentence – 'or'

Task: You must write two compound sentences using the conjunction '**or**'.

Leave a line between each sentence. Each sentence must be punctuated correctly.

Tip: Remember to think about the subject and the verb.

Tip: If you are struggling for inspiration, think about a setting, character or situation from a book you are reading.

Sentence Toolkit Task
Compound Sentence – 'so'

Task: You must write two compound sentences using the conjunction '**so**'.

Leave a line between each sentence. Each sentence must be punctuated correctly.

Tip: Remember to think about the subject and the verb.

Tip: If you are struggling for inspiration, think about a setting, character or situation from a book you are reading.

Sentence Toolkit Task
Compound Sentence – 'for' or 'nor'

Task: You must write two compound sentences using either the conjunction '**for**' or the conjunction '**nor**'.

Leave a line between each sentence. Each sentence must be punctuated correctly.

Tip: Remember to think about the subject and the verb.

Tip: If you are struggling for inspiration, think about a setting, character or situation from a book you are reading.

Sentence Ninja © Andrew Jennings, 2025

SCAFFOLDED FORMATIVE ASSESSMENT PROMPTS

These scaffolded resources provide additional support and advice for pupils.

Sentence Toolkit Task
Compound Sentence – 'and'
Task: You must write two compound sentences using the conjunction '**and**'. Leave a line between each sentence. Each sentence must be punctuated correctly. **Tip:** Remember to think about the subject and the verb.
Conjunction Tip: '**and**' joins two clauses.

Sentence Toolkit Task
Compound Sentence – 'yet'
Task: You must write two compound sentences using the conjunction '**yet**'. Leave a line between each sentence. Each sentence must be punctuated correctly. **Tip:** Remember to think about the subject and the verb.
Conjunction Tip: '**yet**' contrasts two clauses (like 'but').

Sentence Toolkit Task
Compound Sentence – 'but'
Task: You must write two compound sentences using the conjunction '**but**'. Leave a line between each sentence. Each sentence must be punctuated correctly. **Tip:** Remember to think about the subject and the verb.
Conjunction Tip: '**but**' contrasts two clauses.

Sentence Toolkit Task
Compound Sentence – 'or'
Task: You must write two compound sentences using the conjunction '**or**'. Leave a line between each sentence. Each sentence must be punctuated correctly. **Tip:** Remember to think about the subject and the verb.
Conjunction Tip: '**or**' joins two clauses to show two options, alternatives or possibilities.

Sentence Toolkit Task
Compound Sentence – 'so'
Task: You must write two compound sentences using the conjunction '**so**'. Leave a line between each sentence. Each sentence must be punctuated correctly. **Tip:** Remember to think about the subject and the verb.
Conjunction Tip: '**so**' is used to show the result or the 'why?' of the first clause.

Sentence Toolkit Task
Compound Sentence – 'for' or 'nor'
Task: You must write two compound sentences using either the conjunction '**for**' or the conjunction '**nor**'. Leave a line between each sentence. Each sentence must be punctuated correctly. **Tip:** Remember to think about the subject and the verb.
Conjunction Tip: '**nor**' joins two negative clauses and 'for' explains why (like because).

VARIED ASSESSMENT PROMPTS

Varied Assessment Prompts provide a range of assessment activities with varied conjunction and sentence-level expectations. These prompts are ideal for you to use to accurately assess what sentence-level skills your pupils can independently apply.

Sentence Toolkit Task		
Compound Sentences – 'and', 'but', 'so'		
Task: You must write **three** different compound sentences. Each sentence should use one of the three coordinating conjunctions: '**and**', '**but**' and '**so**'.		
Leave a line between each sentence. Each sentence must be punctuated correctly.		
Sentence Checklist (Tick off each sentence as you write.)		and ☐ but ☐ so ☐
Challenge: Once you have completed each sentence, circle the subject and draw a rectangle around the verb in each clause.		

Sentence Toolkit Task		
Compound Sentences – 'yet', 'nor', 'or'		
Task: You must write **three** different compound sentences. Each sentence should use one of the three coordinating conjunctions: '**yet**', '**nor**' and '**or**'.		
Leave a line between each sentence. Each sentence must be punctuated correctly.		
Sentence Checklist (Tick off each sentence as you write.)		yet ☐ nor ☐ or ☐
Challenge: Once you have completed each sentence, circle the subject and draw a rectangle around the verb in each clause.		

Sentence Toolkit Task		
Compound Sentences – 'and', 'but', 'so', 'yet', 'nor', 'or', 'for'		
Task: You must write **seven** different compound sentences. Each sentence should use one of the **seven** coordinating conjunctions: '**and**', '**but**', '**so**', '**yet**', '**nor**', '**or**' and '**for**'.		
Leave a line between each sentence. Each sentence must be punctuated correctly.		
Sentence Checklist (Tick off each sentence as you write.)		and ☐ but ☐ so ☐ yet ☐ nor ☐ or ☐ for ☐
Challenge: Once you have completed each sentence, circle the subject and draw a rectangle around the verb in each clause.		

Sentence Toolkit Task
Sentence-Level Optional Extra – 'however' (Conjunctive Adverb)
Task: You must write **three** different sentences using '**however**'. Remember, '**however**' shows a relationship between two **independent clauses** and transitions from one idea to the next.
Leave a line between each sentence. Each sentence must be punctuated correctly. Remember the **semicolon** and **comma**.
Challenge: Once you have completed each sentence, circle the subject and draw a rectangle around the verb in each clause.

COMPLEX SENTENCES (SUBORDINATING CONJUNCTION)

A note on modal and auxiliary verbs

As sentences become more advanced, they will contain modal verbs (verbs indicating possibility or necessity, such as 'could' and 'should'), and auxiliary verbs (helping verbs, such as 'was' and 'had'), which help the main verb within the sentence to function. For the purposes of this book, we are focusing solely on the main verb.

EXPLICIT MODELLING EXAMPLES AND ACTIVITIES

These examples are purely for teachers and pupils to discuss and explore. Teachers could type these simple sentences on the whiteboard in order to model to pupils how to create a complex sentence with a subject, at least one verb, a conjunction and correct punctuation. Pupils can actively identify the subjects and verbs by circling the subjects and drawing rectangles around the verbs. This can be discussed as part of the modelling. As the teacher types or writes, it is vital to continuously reference clauses as they are created, as well as the conjunction joining them.

As part of the modelling exercise, remember to explain and reinforce what each conjunction is doing and its function in the sentence. See the section on complex sentences for more information (page 45).

Mia was ready to clean the garden **when** Freddy decided to have a nap.
When Freddy decided to have a nap, Mia was ready to clean the garden.
We were going for a walk **when** everyone had finished their lunch.
When everyone had finished their lunch, we were going for a walk.

I will go to the park with you **if** you make the picnic.
If you make the picnic, I will go to the park with you.
The spell needed to work **if** they were going to defeat the ogre.
If they were going to defeat the ogre, the spell needed to work.

Marco wanted to read the whole book **because** the main character was so cool.
Because the main character was so cool, Marco wanted to read the whole book.
The puzzle was finally complete **because** they had found the missing piece.
Because they had found the missing piece, the puzzle was finally complete.

The children were having fun in the puddles **although** it was cold and wet outside.
Although it was cold and wet outside, the children were having fun in the puddles.
The battle was lost **although** they had fought with valour.
Although they had fought with valour, the battle was lost.

Mum packed away the chairs **while** Jeremy finished his sandcastle.
While Jeremy finished his sandcastle, Mum packed away the chairs.
The family huddled together for safety **while** the storm battered the cabin.
While the storm battered the cabin, the family huddled together for safety.

No one could leave the classroom **unless** their table was tidy.
Unless their table was tidy, no one could leave the classroom.
Alice knew she would be late **unless** she could find a shortcut.
Unless she could find a shortcut, Alice knew she would be late.

Sentence Ninja © Andrew Jennings, 2025

DICTATION SENTENCE ACTIVITIES

Sentence-level dictation is an important aspect of low-pressure sentence-level exposure. Dictate the sentences to the pupils, making it clear that the objective is to write a complex sentence, containing two clauses, each with a subject and at least one verb. When each sentence has been written down by the pupils, they should indicate the subject by circling it and the verb by drawing a rectangle around it, before discussing with the teacher what the subject and the verb might be and why. Discussion should also focus around the use of the comma when the subordinate/dependent clause is the first clause of the two.

Every (child) [paused] in silence **when** the (headteacher) [raised] her hand.
When the (headteacher) [raised] her hand, every (child) [paused] in silence.
The (players) [collapsed] to the floor **when** the (referee) [blew] her whistle.
When the (referee) [blew] her whistle, the (players) [collapsed] to the floor.

(I'd) [wish] for fish and chips for tea **if** (I) [had] one wish.
If (I) [had] a one wish, (I'd) [wish] for fish and chips for tea.
(We) will [make] the team **if** (we) [practise] every day.
If (we) [practise] every day, (we) will [make] the team.

(Families) could not [cross] the river **because** the (flood) had [destroyed] the bridge.
Because the (flood) had [destroyed] the bridge, (families) could not [cross] the river.
The (aunties and uncles) [danced] to the music **because** (it) [was] gran's birthday.
Because (it) [was] gran's birthday, the (aunties and uncles) [danced] to the music.

(He) [continued] to swing his sword **although** (he) [was] exhausted.
Although (he) [was] exhausted, (he) [continued] to swing his sword.
The (end of the book) [was] exciting **although** (I) already [knew] how it ended.
Although (I) already [knew] how it ended, the (end of the book) [was] exciting.

(Firefighters) [arrived] to tackle the blaze **while** (fire) [engulfed] the building.
While (fire) [engulfed] the building, (firefighters) [arrived] to tackle the blaze.
His tired (dog) [snoozed] on the sofa **while** (Andrew) [watched] television.
While (Andrew) [watched] television, his tired (dog) [snoozed] on the sofa.

The evil (wizard) [refused] to release them **unless** (they) [collected] enough gold.
Unless (they) [collected] enough gold, the evil (wizard) [refused] to release them.
(Water) would [spill] over onto the floor **unless** (they) [turned] the tap off.
Unless (they) [turned] the tap off, (water) would [spill] over onto the floor.

COMPLETE THE SENTENCE

These activities require pupils to complete the sentences by adding the additional clauses. The words they add will need to include a subject and a verb. Pupils should be encouraged to punctuate the clauses accurately with a full stop to form a complete, complex sentence. Pupils should also circle the subjects and draw rectangles around the verbs. Attention to where and when the comma should be used is crucial, depending on where the subordinate/dependent clause is positioned.

Complete and punctuate each clause to make a complex sentence.

The children came in from the playground **when** _____

When the red car pulled over, _____

Everyone clapped and cheered loudly **when** _____

Complete and punctuate each clause to make a complex sentence.

Janet was going to win the spelling bee **if** _____

If there weren't enough seats, _____

The dog wouldn't wake up **if** _____

Complete and punctuate each clause to make a complex sentence.

Because the fire alarm started to ring, _____

Billy stacked his books neatly **because** _____

Because of the thick fog, _____

Complete and punctuate each clause to make a complex sentence.

Although he was going to crash, _____

Jimmy continued to eat more food **although** _____

Although the cup of tea was cold, _____

Complete and punctuate each clause to make a complex sentence.

While Andy got dressed for the party, _____

The cat walked along the top of the fence **while** _____

Mum hoovered inside the car **while** _____

Complete and punctuate each clause to make a complex sentence.

Freya wasn't allowed to leave the dinner table **unless** _____

Unless the mystery gang could crack the code, _____

The equipment would run out of power **unless** _____

COMPLETE THE SENTENCE

Complete and punctuate each clause to make a complex sentence.

Alice watched on in complete shock **when** _____

The owl swooped down from the tree **because** _____

We can improve our writing **if** _____

Complete and punctuate each clause to make a complex sentence.

When the asteroid landed in the ocean, _____

Because the fly landed on her arm, _____

If the twins would just stop arguing, _____

Complete and punctuate each clause to make a complex sentence.

The sheep started to run away **when** _____

None of the children wanted to play football anymore **because** _____

They would be able to get new bikes **if** _____

Complete and punctuate each clause to make a complex sentence.

When Alex discovered his old skateboard, _____

Because of the beautiful, sunny weather, _____

If one more person shouts out, _____

Complete and punctuate each clause to make a complex sentence.

Freddy was ready to leave **when** _____

Marco rushed his painting **because** _____

Everyone could have the day off school **if** _____

Complete and punctuate each clause to make a complex sentence.

When the food was cool enough to eat, _____

Because I wasn't willing to share, _____

If Timmy was a little bit taller, _____

COMPLETE THE SENTENCE

Complete and punctuate each clause to make a complex sentence.
Jeremy told Mia that he was sorry **although** _____
Alexia sketched the flowers in the forest **while** _____
Freddy wouldn't give John a turn **unless** _____

Complete and punctuate each clause to make a complex sentence.
Although they had run out of time, _____
While the boys played with their toys, _____
Unless someone told the truth, _____

Complete and punctuate each clause to make a complex sentence.
Alex filled up all of the water bottles **although** _____
Mr Johnson read the class a story **while** _____
There was no way to learn the whole song **unless** _____

Complete and punctuate each clause to make a complex sentence.
Although Jess was a great friend, _____
While they waited for the waiter, _____
Unless the weather improved, _____

Complete and punctuate each clause to make a complex sentence.
They would not be going again **although** _____
We all laughed **while** _____
Robert couldn't chop more wood **unless** _____

Complete and punctuate each clause to make a complex sentence.
Although the fire was keeping them warm, _____
While James had a well-deserved drink of water, _____
Unless Mia could find her helmet, _____

COMPLETE THE SENTENCE

Complete and punctuate each clause to make a complex sentence.

All of the fans rushed onto the pitch **when** _____

Mark said it had been the best day **because** _____

The art lesson would be extended **if** _____

Our writing was going to be read out in the assembly **although** _____

The beaver collected sticks for the dam **while** _____

The beach would always be full of litter **unless** _____

Complete and punctuate each clause to make a complex sentence.

When the doors of the Higgins boat opened, _____

Because Mia hadn't packed the right equipment, _____

If we want to go on the new rollercoaster, _____

Although I'm scared of heights, _____

While everyone else was messing around, _____

Unless our friends come to help us, _____

Complete and punctuate each clause to make a complex sentence.

When the seagull stole our chips, _____

Alex came to school in fancy dress **because** _____

If they didn't call the coastguard right now, _____

The beans on toast were very tasty **although** _____

While the hawk watched from the sky above, _____

The parents were not allowed to help **unless** _____

CLAUSE COMBINING

Below are 8 independent clauses. Add the subordinating conjunctions to create subordinate/dependent clauses and then join them to the independent clauses. Write out 4 complete sentences. Each conjunction should only be used once. Remember to punctuate the sentences.

when	if	because	although
Independent clause		**Make dependent by adding conjunction**	
we couldn't play tennis		the train arrived into the station	
Danny loved reading that book		she had been ill all day	
there was a small cheer		the grass hadn't been cut	
Freya wasn't coming to the party		he had already read it many times	

Below are 8 independent clauses. Add the subordinating conjunctions to create subordinate/dependent clauses and then join them to the independent clauses. Write out 4 complete sentences. Each conjunction should only be used once. Remember to punctuate the sentences.

while	unless	because	when
Independent clause		**Make dependent by adding conjunction**	
she was awarded three marks		the film had finished	
Tia played on her phone		it was handed in on time	
Tim and Mia had to go to bed		she had her hair cut	
the competition entry wouldn't be accepted		she showed her working out	

Below are 8 independent clauses. Add the subordinating conjunctions to create subordinate/dependent clauses and then join them to the independent clauses. Write out 4 complete sentences. Each conjunction should only be used once. Remember to punctuate the sentences.

if	although	while	unless
Independent clause		**Make dependent by adding conjunction**	
the rabbit chewed the grass		he didn't have many subscribers	
there was nothing he could do to win		he was prepared to cheat	
John posted another new video		she could have five more minutes to read	
she promised to wash the car		the predator watched from the shadows	

Below are 8 independent clauses. Add the subordinating conjunctions to create subordinate/dependent clauses and then join them to the independent clauses. Write out 4 complete sentences. Each conjunction should only be used once. Remember to punctuate the sentences.

because	if	unless	when
Independent clause		**Make dependent by adding conjunction**	
the explorer decided to build a shelter		she didn't agree with them	
Mia was prepared to be captain		no one else was brave enough to do it	
John ordered a vegetable pizza		the sky started to become dark	
Petra always followed instructions		it was his favourite meal	

PRINTABLE PROMPTS

Print, cut and stick these sentence challenges into your pupils' books. Encourage pupils to create specific complex sentences and to consider the role of the conjunction in each sentence, as well as the presence of the subject and the main verb in each clause.

'when' – Sentence Challenge

Write three separate sentences using '**when**' as a subordinating conjunction.

At least one of your sentences should vary your clause structure and start with the dependent/subordinate clause.

Remember that '**when**' means '**at that time**'.

Each clause should contain a subject and a verb.

When you have finished each sentence, underline the conjunction, circle the subject and draw a rectangle around the verb in each clause.

'if' – Sentence Challenge

Write three separate sentences using '**if**' as a subordinating conjunction.

At least one of your sentences should vary your clause structure and start with the dependent/subordinate clause.

Remember that '**if' shows a condition which something else depends on.**

Each clause should contain a subject and a verb.

When you have finished each sentence, underline the conjunction, circle the subject and draw a rectangle around the verb in each clause.

'because' – Sentence Challenge

Write three separate sentences using '**because**' as a subordinating conjunction.

At least one of your sentences should vary your clause structure and start with the dependent/subordinate clause.

Remember that '**because' explains a reason or cause.**

Each clause should contain a subject and a verb.

When you have finished each sentence, underline the conjunction, circle the subject and draw a rectangle around the verb in each clause.

'although' – Sentence Challenge

Write three separate sentences using '**although**' as a subordinating conjunction.

At least one of your sentences should vary your clause structure and start with the dependent/subordinate clause.

Remember that '**although' connects contrasting or contradictory information.**

Each clause should contain a subject and a verb.

When you have finished each sentence, underline the conjunction, circle the subject and draw a rectangle around the verb in each clause.

'while' – Sentence Challenge

Write three separate sentences using '**while**' as a subordinating conjunction.

At least one of your sentences should vary your clause structure and start with the dependent/subordinate clause.

Remember that '**while' shows an action or event, as another is happening.**

Each clause should contain a subject and a verb.

When you have finished each sentence, underline the conjunction, circle the subject and draw a rectangle around the verb in each clause.

'unless' – Sentence Challenge

Write three separate sentences using '**unless**' as a subordinating conjunction.

At least one of your sentences should vary your clause structure and start with the dependent/subordinate clause.

Remember that '**unless' shows that something will or will not happen 'unless' another action happens or condition is met.**

Each clause should contain a subject and a verb.

When you have finished each sentence, underline the conjunction, circle the subject and draw a rectangle around the verb in each clause.

FORMATIVE ASSESSMENT PROMPTS

The resources found on the following pages can be used within a classroom or across the whole school to assess and track pupils' sentence-level skill. The prompts are relatively simple prompts, which ask pupils to write specific sentence types that require the pupils to demonstrate their ability to create those particular sentence types.

These can be completed easily and within a short time period of around five minutes. It is advisable to make this assessment extremely informal, to the point where the pupils see it as just another task, rather than an assessment. The information gleaned from the assessments will help teachers to better understand and track the depth and wealth of each pupil's sentence-level toolkit.

Sentence Toolkit Task

Complex Sentence – 'when'

Task: You must write two compound sentences using the conjunction '**when**'.

Leave a line between each sentence. Each sentence must be punctuated correctly.

Tip: Remember to think about the subject and the verb.

Tip: If you are struggling for inspiration, think about a setting, character or situation from a book you are reading.

Sentence Toolkit Task

Complex Sentence – 'if'

Task: You must write two compound sentences using the conjunction '**if**'.

Leave a line between each sentence. Each sentence must be punctuated correctly.

Tip: Remember to think about the subject and the verb.

Tip: If you are struggling for inspiration, think about a setting, character or situation from a book you are reading.

Sentence Toolkit Task

Complex Sentence – 'because'

Task: You must write two compound sentences using the conjunction '**because**'.

Leave a line between each sentence. Each sentence must be punctuated correctly.

Tip: Remember to think about the subject and the verb.

Tip: If you are struggling for inspiration, think about a setting, character or situation from a book you are reading.

Sentence Toolkit Task

Complex Sentence – 'although'

Task: You must write two compound sentences using the conjunction '**although**'.

Leave a line between each sentence. Each sentence must be punctuated correctly.

Tip: Remember to think about the subject and the verb.

Tip: If you are struggling for inspiration, think about a setting, character or situation from a book you are reading.

Sentence Toolkit Task

Complex Sentence – 'while'

Task: You must write two compound sentences using the conjunction '**while**'.

Leave a line between each sentence. Each sentence must be punctuated correctly.

Tip: Remember to think about the subject and the verb.

Tip: If you are struggling for inspiration, think about a setting, character or situation from a book you are reading.

Sentence Toolkit Task

Complex Sentence – 'unless'

Task: You must write two compound sentences using the conjunction '**unless**'.

Leave a line between each sentence. Each sentence must be punctuated correctly.

Tip: Remember to think about the subject and the verb.

Tip: If you are struggling for inspiration, think about a setting, character or situation from a book you are reading.

SCAFFOLDED FORMATIVE ASSESSMENT PROMPTS

These scaffolded resources provide additional support and advice for pupils.

Sentence Toolkit Task

Compound Sentence – 'when'

Task: You must write two compound sentences using the conjunction '**when**'.

Leave a line between each sentence. Each sentence must be punctuated correctly.

Tip: Remember to think about the subject and the verb.

Tip: Think about your clause structure and if certain punctuation is required or not.

Tip: If you are struggling for inspiration, think about a setting, character or situation from a book you are reading.

Conjunction Tip: '**when**' means 'at that time'.

Sentence Toolkit Task

Compound Sentence – 'if'

Task: You must write two compound sentences using the conjunction '**if**'.

Leave a line between each sentence. Each sentence must be punctuated correctly.

Tip: Remember to think about the subject and the verb.

Tip: Think about your clause structure and if certain punctuation is required or not.

Tip: If you are struggling for inspiration, think about a setting, character or situation from a book you are reading.

Conjunction Tip: '**if**' shows a condition which something else depends on.

Sentence Toolkit Task

Compound Sentence – 'because'

Task: You must write two compound sentences using the conjunction '**because**'.

Leave a line between each sentence. Each sentence must be punctuated correctly.

Tip: Remember to think about the subject and the verb.

Tip: Think about your clause structure and if certain punctuation is required or not.

Tip: If you are struggling for inspiration, think about a setting, character or situation from a book you are reading.

Conjunction Tip: '**because**' explains a reason or cause.

Sentence Toolkit Task

Compound Sentence – 'although'

Task: You must write two compound sentences using the conjunction '**although**'.

Leave a line between each sentence. Each sentence must be punctuated correctly.

Tip: Remember to think about the subject and the verb.

Tip: Think about your clause structure and if certain punctuation is required or not.

Tip: If you are struggling for inspiration, think about a setting, character or situation from a book you are reading.

Conjunction Tip: '**although**' connects contrasting or contradictory information.

Sentence Toolkit Task

Compound Sentence – 'while'

Task: You must write two compound sentences using the conjunction '**while**'.

Leave a line between each sentence. Each sentence must be punctuated correctly.

Tip: Remember to think about the subject and the verb.

Tip: Think about your clause structure and if certain punctuation is required or not.

Tip: If you are struggling for inspiration, think about a setting, character or situation from a book you are reading.

Conjunction Tip: '**while**' shows an action or event, as another is happening.

Sentence Toolkit Task

Compound Sentence – 'unless'

Task: You must write two compound sentences using the conjunction '**unless**'.

Leave a line between each sentence. Each sentence must be punctuated correctly.

Tip: Remember to think about the subject and the verb.

Tip: Think about your clause structure and if certain punctuation is required or not.

Tip: If you are struggling for inspiration, think about a setting, character or situation from a book you are reading.

Conjunction Tip: '**unless**' shows that something will or will not happen 'unless' another action happens or condition is met.

VARIED ASSESSMENT PROMPTS

Varied Assessment Prompts provide a range of assessment activities with varied conjunctions and sentence-level expectations. These prompts are ideal for you to use to accurately assess what sentence-level skills your pupils can independently apply.

Sentence Toolkit Task	
Compound Sentences – 'when', 'if', 'because'	
Task: You must write **three** different compound sentences. Each sentence should use one of the three subordinating conjunctions '**when**', '**if**' and '**because**'. Leave a line between each sentence. Remember to punctuate each sentence.	
Sentence Checklist (Tick off each sentence as you write.)	when ☐ if ☐ because ☐
Challenge: Once you have completed each sentence, circle the subject in each clause and draw a rectangle around the verb.	

Sentence Toolkit Task	
Compound Sentences – 'although', 'while', 'unless'	
Task: You must write **three** different compound sentences. Each sentence should use one of the three subordinating conjunctions '**although**', '**while**' and '**unless**'. Leave a line between each sentence. Remember to punctuate each sentence.	
Sentence Checklist (Tick off each sentence as you write.)	although ☐ while ☐ unless ☐
Challenge: Once you have completed each sentence, circle the subject in each clause and draw a rectangle around the verb.	

Sentence Toolkit Task	
Compound Sentences – 'when', 'while', 'because'	
Task: You must write **three** different compound sentences. Each sentence should use one of the three subordinating conjunctions '**when**', '**while**' and '**because**'. Leave a line between each sentence. Remember to punctuate each sentence.	
Sentence Checklist (Tick off each sentence as you write.)	when ☐ while ☐ because ☐
Challenge: Once you have completed each sentence, circle the subject in each clause and draw a rectangle around the verb.	

Sentence Toolkit Task	
Compound Sentences – 'if', 'although', 'unless'	
Task: You must write **three** different compound sentences. Each sentence should use one of the three subordinating conjunctions '**if**', '**although**' and '**unless**'. Leave a line between each sentence. Remember to punctuate each sentence.	
Sentence Checklist (Tick off each sentence as you write.)	if ☐ although ☐ unless ☐
Challenge: Once you have completed each sentence, circle the subject in each clause and draw a rectangle around the verb.	

Sentence Toolkit Task	
Complex Sentences – 'when', 'if', 'because' 'although', 'while', 'unless'	
Task: You must write **six** different complex sentences. Each sentence should use one of the **six** subordinating conjunctions '**when**', '**if**', '**because**' '**although**', '**while**', and '**unless**'. Leave a line between each sentence. Remember to punctuate each sentence.	
Sentence Checklist (Tick off each sentence as you write.)	when ☐ if ☐ because ☐ although ☐ while ☐ unless ☐
Challenge: Once you have completed each sentence, circle the subject in each clause and draw a rectangle around the verb.	

Sentence Ninja © Andrew Jennings, 2025

RELATIVE CLAUSES (RELATIVE PRONOUN)

A note on modal and auxiliary verbs

As sentences become more advanced, they will contain modal verbs (verbs indicating possibility or necessity, such as 'could' and 'should'), and auxiliary verbs (helping verbs, such as 'was' and 'had'), which help the main verb within the sentence to function. For the purposes of this book, we are focusing solely on the main verb.

EXPLICIT MODELLING EXAMPLES AND ACTIVITIES

These examples are purely for teachers and pupils to discuss and explore. Teachers could type these simple sentences on the whiteboard in order to model to pupils how to create a sentence using a specific relative clause. This discussion and modelling should focus on the use of the relative pronoun, the clause structure and the subject and the main verb. As the teacher types or writes, it is vital to continuously reference this information.

> **Remember:** When should you use a comma to mark a relative clause?
>
> **Essential:** An essential relative clause provides crucial information about the noun it modifies and so it is necessary for the sentence's meaning. So, a comma **is not** used.
>
> **Non-Essential:** If the information being added by the relative clause is not essential for the meaning of the sentence, a comma **is** used.

essential	I have a friend **who** lives in Newcastle.
essential	She is the doctor **who** treated my friend.
non-essential	We love to visit our grandparents, **who** live in a small cottage.
non-essential	The dog barked at my mum, **who** was terrified.

essential	I need the book **which** is on the top shelf.
essential	She chose the dress **which** fit her perfectly.
non-essential	Mia loved eating her mum's cupcakes, **which** were full of jam.
non-essential	Freddy got a new football kit, **which** was red and blue.

essential	I met the author **whose** book I had read.
essential	We hired the teacher **whose** qualities were outstanding.
non-essential	Mia shouted at Alice, **whose** shoelace was loose.
non-essential	I love listening to Mrs Roberts, **whose** voice is magical.

essential	Freddy showed us the house **where** he grew up.
essential	She showed me the room **where** the art supplies were kept.
non-essential	We stayed in a hotel, **where** the service was excellent.
non-essential	We went to the local beach, **where** we built sandcastles.

essential	She likes to walk in the evening **when** the weather is cool.
essential	We always have a nice barbeque **when** it's sunny outside.
non-essential	We had a great time at the party, **when** the music was playing.
non-essential	The children played in the garden, **when** the rain had stopped.

essential	I need to return the book **that** I borrowed from the library.
essential	It was finally the day **that** everyone had been waiting for.
non-essential	*Note – 'that' is never used to introduce a non-essential clause.*
non-essential	*Note – 'that' is never used to introduce a non-essential clause.*

Sentence Ninja © Andrew Jennings, 2025

DICTATION SENTENCE ACTIVITIES

Sentence-level dictation is an important aspect of low-pressure sentence-level exposure. Teachers should dictate the sentences to the pupils, making it clear that the objective is to write a sentence containing a relative clause.

When each sentence has been written by pupils, they should indicate the subject by drawing a circle around it, and the main verb by drawing a rectangle around it, before discussing with the teacher what the subject and verb might be and why. Discussion should also focus on the use of the relative pronoun, the clause and the comma, depending on whether the relative clause is **essential** or **non-essential**.

Essential Clauses

'I bought the laptop that has the latest processor.'

Teacher Explanation

In this sentence, the relative clause 'that has the latest processor' is essential because it specifies which laptop the speaker bought. Without this information, it would be unclear which laptop is being referred to among all the available options. So, the relative clause is essential for understanding the sentence's meaning.

'She chose the dress that fitted her perfectly'

Teacher Explanation

Here, the relative clause 'that fitted her perfectly' is essential because it identifies which dress she chose. This information is crucial for understanding the context of the sentence and which dress she selected among various options.

'We visited the museum that houses ancient artefacts.'

Teacher Explanation

In this sentence, the relative clause 'that houses ancient artefacts' is essential because it specifies which museum the speaker visited. Without this information, it would be ambiguous which museum is being referred to among all possible museums. So, the relative clause is essential for understanding the sentence's meaning.

Non-Essential Clauses

'We went to the beach, where we built sandcastles'

Teacher Explanation

In this sentence, the relative clause 'where we built sandcastles' is non-essential because it provides additional information about the beach but is not necessary to identify which beach the speaker went to. The main point of the sentence is that the speaker went to the beach.

'He attended the concert, where he met his favourite singer.'

Teacher Explanation

Here, the relative clause 'where he met his favourite singer' is non-essential because it adds extra detail about the concert but is not crucial for understanding which concert he attended. The main point of the sentence is that he attended a concert.

'She visited the city, where she explored the historic landmarks'

Teacher Explanation

In this sentence, the relative clause 'where she explored the historic landmarks' is non-essential because it provides additional information about the city but is not necessary for identifying which city she visited. The main point of the sentence is that she visited a city.

COMPLETE THE SENTENCE

These activities require pupils to complete the sentence by adding a relative clause. Pupils should be encouraged to make an active and conscious decision about whether or not the relative clause being added is essential or non-essential. If it is **essential**, there should **not** be a comma. If the relative clause is **non-essential**, there **should** be a comma.

Complete and punctuate each sentence with a relative clause – 'who'.
Tip: If we expand the noun with an essential relative clause, then we don't need a comma. If the extension is non-essential, then we will need to use a comma.
Alice loved to spend time with Pearl _____
She said thank you to the firefighter _____
Everyone was pleased to see Uncle Malik _____

Complete and punctuate each sentence with a relative clause – 'which'.
Tip: If we expand the noun with an essential relative clause, then we don't need a comma. If the extension is non-essential, then we will need to use a comma.
She rubbed dirt from the ancient coin _____
The family boarded the huge aeroplane _____
Dad tried to stretch out his back _____

Complete and punctuate each sentence with a relative clause – 'whose'.
Tip: If we expand the noun with an essential relative clause, then we don't need a comma. If the extension is non-essential, then we will need to use a comma.
Everyone was worried after what happened to Mia _____
The mood was low for the whole team _____
Dad bought a present to surprise Daniel _____

Complete and punctuate each sentence with a relative clause – 'where'.
Tip: If we expand the noun with an essential relative clause, then we don't need a comma. If the extension is non-essential, then we will need to use a comma.
Tia was reluctant to go back to the museum _____
Jen and Thea couldn't wait to get to the tennis courts _____
Dad was excited to visit his favourite restaurant _____

Complete and punctuate each sentence with a relative clause – 'when'.
Tip: If we expand the noun with an essential relative clause, then we don't need a comma. If the extension is non-essential, then we will need to use a comma.
Mum loved to walk the dog at night _____
We decided to cancel our trip to the beach _____
The owl swooped down silently from the tree _____

Complete and punctuate each sentence with a relative clause – 'that'.
Tip: If we expand the noun with an essential relative clause, then we don't need a comma. If the extension is non-essential, then we will need to use a comma.
The dog ate the picnic _____
Our garden was full of busy ants _____
The headteacher needed to make an announcement _____

COMPLETE THE SENTENCE

In the following activities, pupils need to focus on the noun that the first clause ends in, which we can see in **bold**. This noun will determine which pronoun pupils can potentially use. For example, if the noun is a name or a person, we would likely use the relative pronoun '**who**' to expand on the noun.

A further consideration is how pupils expand the sentence. If they expand the noun with an essential relative clause, then a comma **is not** needed. If the extension is non-essential, then a comma **is** needed. Try to encourage pupils to make a conscious and active decision here; ultimately, the sentence needs to read well.

We managed to catch the **bus** _____
The crowd gathered outside the **stadium** _____
I met a new **friend** _____
We visited a **museum** _____
She has a beautiful new **bag** _____
I saw a huge **eagle** _____
They have a large **garden** _____
We found a mysterious **coin** _____
He bought some **sweets** _____
I know a famous **footballer** _____

We all fell out of the old **treehouse** _____
I didn't know how to heal my broken **heart** _____
I wanted to visit **Australia** _____
We spent time at the **playground** _____
She washed her **hair** _____
I read a very interesting **book** _____
They always bring tasty **sandwiches** _____
We adopted a cute **puppy** _____
He destroyed his **model** _____
I love staring out of the **window** _____

We laughed at the **jokes** _____
The geese were making a loud **noise** _____
I had always wanted to see **Buckingham Palace** _____
We spent hours just watching the **clouds** _____
She was new at our **school** _____
I was jealous of how good she was at **chess** _____
They spent time growing **vegetables** _____
She was going out with her **friends** _____
He knew it was a bad **decision** _____
I like to play on my **games console** _____

PRINTABLE PROMPTS

Print, cut and stick these sentence challenges into your pupils' books. Encourage pupils to create specific sentences that use a relative clause. When they have written their sentences, the role the relative pronoun plays in each sentence, as well as the presence of the subject and the main verb in each clause and the use of punctuation, should be discussed with the pupils.

'who' – Relative Clause Challenge

Write three separate sentences using '**who**' as a relative pronoun.

Remember to think about whether the relative clause is **essential** (no comma) or **non-essential** (comma).

Each sentence should be punctuated correctly.

When you have finished each sentence, underline the relative pronoun, circle the subject and draw a rectangle around the verb in each clause.

'which' – Relative Clause Challenge

Write three separate sentences using '**which**' as a relative pronoun.

Remember to think about whether the relative clause is **essential** (no comma) or **non-essential** (comma).

Each sentence should be punctuated correctly.

When you have finished each sentence, underline the relative pronoun, circle the subject and draw a rectangle around the verb in each clause.

'that' – Relative Clause Challenge

Write three separate sentences using '**that**' as a relative pronoun.

Remember, 'that' can only be used to introduce an **essential clause** (no comma).

Each sentence should be punctuated correctly.

When you have finished each sentence, underline the relative pronoun, circle the subject and draw a rectangle around the verb in each clause.

'whose' – Relative Clause Challenge

Write three separate sentences using '**whose**' as a relative pronoun.

Remember to think about whether the relative clause is **essential** (no comma) or **non-essential** (comma).

Each sentence should be punctuated correctly.

When you have finished each sentence, underline the relative pronoun, circle the subject and draw a rectangle around the verb in each clause.

'where' – Relative Clause Challenge

Write three separate sentences using '**where**' as a relative pronoun.

Remember to think about whether the relative clause is **essential** (no comma) or **non-essential** (comma).

Each sentence should be punctuated correctly.

When you have finished each sentence, underline the relative pronoun, circle the subject and draw a rectangle around the verb in each clause.

'when' – Relative Clause Challenge

Write three separate sentences using '**when**' as a relative pronoun.

Remember to think about whether the relative clause is **essential** (no comma) or **non-essential** (comma).

Each sentence should be punctuated correctly.

When you have finished each sentence, underline the relative pronoun, circle the subject and draw a rectangle around the verb in each clause.

FORMATIVE ASSESSMENT PROMPTS

The resources found on the following pages can be used within a classroom or across the whole school to assess and track pupils' sentence-level skill. The prompts are relatively simple prompts, which ask pupils to write specific sentence types that require the pupils to demonstrate their ability to create those particular sentence types.

These can be completed easily and within a short time period of around five minutes. It is advisable to make this assessment extremely informal, to the point where the pupils see it as just another task, rather than an assessment. The information gleaned from the assessments will help teachers to better understand and track the depth and wealth of each pupil's sentence-level toolkit.

Sentence Toolkit Task

Relative Clause – 'who'

Task: You must write three sentences that contain a relative clause, using the relative pronoun '**who**'.

Leave a line between each sentence. Each sentence must be punctuated correctly.

Tip: Remember to think about the subject and the verb.

Sentence Toolkit Task

Relative Clause – 'which'

Task: You must write three sentences that contain a relative clause, using the relative pronoun '**which**'.

Leave a line between each sentence. Each sentence must be punctuated correctly.

Tip: Remember to think about the subject and the verb.

Sentence Toolkit Task

Relative Clause – 'that'

Task: You must write three sentences that contain a relative clause, using the relative pronoun '**that**'.

Leave a line between each sentence. Each sentence must be punctuated correctly.

Tip: Remember to think about the subject and the verb.

Sentence Toolkit Task

Relative Clause – 'whose'

Task: You must write three sentences that contain a relative clause, using the relative pronoun '**whose**'.

Leave a line between each sentence. Each sentence must be punctuated correctly.

Tip: Remember to think about the subject and the verb.

Sentence Toolkit Task

Relative Clause – 'where'

Task: You must write three sentences that contain a relative clause, using the relative pronoun '**where**'.

Leave a line between each sentence. Each sentence must be punctuated correctly.

Tip: Remember to think about the subject and the verb.

Sentence Toolkit Task

Relative Clause – 'when'

Task: You must write three sentences that contain a relative clause, using the relative pronoun '**when**'.

Leave a line between each sentence. Each sentence must be punctuated correctly.

Tip: Remember to think about the subject and the verb.

SCAFFOLDED FORMATIVE ASSESSMENT PROMPTS

These scaffolded resources provide additional support and advice for pupils.

Sentence Toolkit Task
Relative Clause – 'who'
Task: You must write three sentences that contain a relative clause, using the relative pronoun '**who**'. Leave a line between each sentence. Each sentence must be punctuated correctly.
Tip: Remember to think about the subject and the verb.
Tip: Think about a setting, character or situation from a book you are reading if you are struggling for inspiration.
Tip: If the relative clause is **essential**, there should **not** be a comma. If the clause is **non-essential**, there **should** be a comma.

Sentence Toolkit Task
Relative Clause – 'which'
Task: You must write three sentences that contain a relative clause, using the relative pronoun '**which**'. Leave a line between each sentence. Each sentence must be punctuated correctly.
Tip: Remember to think about the subject and the verb.
Tip: Think about a setting, character or situation from a book you are reading if you are struggling for inspiration.
Tip: If the relative clause is **essential**, there should **not** be a comma. If the clause is **non-essential**, there **should** be a comma.

Sentence Toolkit Task
Relative Clause – 'that'
Task: You must write three sentences that contain a relative clause, using the relative pronoun '**that**'. Leave a line between each sentence. Each sentence must be punctuated correctly.
Tip: Remember to think about the subject and the verb.
Tip: Think about a setting, character or situation from a book you are reading if you are struggling for inspiration.
Tip: 'That' can only be used to introduce an **essential** clause (no comma).

Sentence Toolkit Task
Relative Clause – 'when'
Task: You must write three sentences that contain a relative clause, using the relative pronoun '**when**'. Leave a line between each sentence. Each sentence must be punctuated correctly.
Tip: Remember to think about the subject and the verb.
Tip: Think about a setting, character or situation from a book you are reading if you are struggling for inspiration.
Tip: If the relative clause is **essential**, there should **not** be a comma. If the clause is **non-essential**, there **should** be a comma.

Sentence Toolkit Task
Relative Clause – 'where'
Task: You must write three sentences that contain a relative clause, using the relative pronoun '**where**'. Leave a line between each sentence. Each sentence must be punctuated correctly.
Tip: Remember to think about the subject and the verb.
Tip: Think about a setting, character or situation from a book you are reading if you are struggling for inspiration.
Tip: If the relative clause is **essential**, there should **not** be a comma. If the clause is **non-essential**, there **should** be a comma.

Sentence Toolkit Task
Relative Clause – 'when'
Task: You must write three sentences that contain a relative clause, using the relative pronoun '**when**'. Leave a line between each sentence. Each sentence must be punctuated correctly.
Tip: Remember to think about the subject and the verb.
Tip: Think about a setting, character or situation from a book you are reading if you are struggling for inspiration.
Tip: If the relative clause is **essential**, there should **not** be a comma. If the clause is **non-essential**, there **should** be a comma.

VARIED ASSESSMENT PROMPTS

Varied Assessment Prompts provide a range of assessment activities with varied conjunctions and sentence-level expectations. These prompts are ideal for you to use to accurately assess what sentence-level skills your pupils can independently apply.

Sentence Toolkit Task	
Relative Clauses – 'who', 'which', 'that'	
Task: You must write three sentences that contain a relative clause. Each sentence should use one of the following relative pronouns: '**who**', '**which**' and '**that**'. Leave a line between each sentence. Remember to punctuate each sentence. **Tip:** If the relative clause is **essential**, there should **not** be a comma. If the clause is **non-essential**, there **should** be a comma.	
Sentence Checklist (Tick off each sentence as you write.)	who ☐ which ☐ that ☐
Challenge: Once you have completed each sentence, circle the subject and draw a rectangle around the verb in each clause.	

Sentence Toolkit Task	
Relative Clauses – 'whose', 'where', 'when'	
Task: You must write three sentences that contain a relative clause. Each sentence should use one of the following relative pronouns: '**whose**', '**where**' and '**when**'. Leave a line between each sentence. Remember to punctuate each sentence. **Tip:** If the relative clause is **essential**, there should **not** be a comma. If the clause is **non-essential**, there **should** be a comma.	
Sentence Checklist (Tick off each sentence as you write.)	whose ☐ where ☐ when ☐
Challenge: Once you have completed each sentence, circle the subject and draw a rectangle around the verb in each clause.	

Sentence Toolkit Task	
Relative Clauses – 'where', 'who', 'whose'	
Task: You must write three sentences that contain a relative clause. Each sentence should use one of the following relative pronouns: '**where**', '**who**' and '**whose**'. Leave a line between each sentence. Remember to punctuate each sentence. **Tip:** If the relative clause is **essential**, there should **not** be a comma. If the clause is **non-essential**, there **should** be a comma.	
Sentence Checklist (Tick off each sentence as you write.)	where ☐ who ☐ whose ☐
Challenge: Once you have completed each sentence, circle the subject and draw a rectangle around the verb in each clause.	

Sentence Toolkit Task	
Relative Clauses – 'which', 'that', 'where'	
Task: You must write three sentences that contain a relative clause. Each sentence should use one of the following relative pronouns: '**which**', '**that**' and '**where**'. Leave a line between each sentence. Remember to punctuate each sentence. **Tip:** If the relative clause is **essential**, there should **not** be a comma. If the clause is **non-essential**, there **should** be a comma.	
Sentence Checklist (Tick off each sentence as you write.)	which ☐ that ☐ where ☐
Challenge: Once you have completed each sentence, circle the subject and draw a rectangle around the verb in each clause.	

Sentence Toolkit Task	
Relative Clauses – 'who', 'which', 'that', 'whose', 'where', 'when'	
Task: You must write **six** different sentences that use a relative clause beginning with a relative pronoun. Each sentence should use one of the **six** relative pronouns: '**who**', '**which**', '**that**', '**whose**', '**where**' and '**when**'. Leave a line between each sentence. Remember to punctuate each sentence. **Tip:** If the relative clause is **essential**, there should **not** be a comma. If the clause is **non-essential**, there **should** be a comma.	
Sentence Checklist (Tick off each sentence as you write.)	who ☐ which ☐ that ☐ whose ☐ where ☐ when ☐
Challenge: Once you have completed each sentence, circle the subject and draw a rectangle around the verb in each clause.	

RELATIVE EMBEDDED CLAUSES

A note on modal and auxiliary verbs

As sentences become more advanced, they will contain modal verbs (verbs indicating possibility or necessity, such as 'could' and 'should'), and auxiliary verbs (helping verbs, such as 'was' and 'had'), which help the main verb within the sentence to function. For the purposes of this book, we are focusing solely on the main verb.

EXPLICIT MODELLING EXAMPLES AND ACTIVITIES

These examples are purely for teachers and pupils to discuss and explore. Teachers could type these simple sentences on the whiteboard in order to model to pupils how to create a sentence using a specific relative clause. This discussion and modelling should focus on the use of the relative pronoun, the clause structure and the subject and the main verb. As the teacher types or writes, it is vital to continuously reference this information.

Remember: When should you use commas to mark an embedded relative clause?

Essential: An essential relative clause provides crucial information about the noun it modifies and so it is necessary for the sentence's meaning. So, commas **are not** used.

Non-Essential: If the information being added by the relative clause **is not** essential for the meaning of the sentence, commas **are** used.

essential	The **person who won the competition** will receive a prize.
essential	The dog **who barks at strangers** belongs to our neighbour.
non-essential	My friend**, who loves to travel,** is planning a trip to Asia.
non-essential	The chef**, who has won several awards,** prepared our meal.

essential	The restaurant **which serves sushi** is my favourite.
essential	The car **which has a flat tire** needs to be repaired.
non-essential	We visited the museum**, which was founded in 1920,** last weekend.
non-essential	The cat**, which is black,** loves to sleep in the sun.

essential	The **car that I bought last year** broke down.
essential	The person **that I spoke to on the phone** was very helpful.
non-essential	My pencil**, that I use in school,** is very sharp.
non-essential	The laptop**, that has a touch screen,** is very expensive.

essential	The girl **whose mother is a doctor** won the science competition.
essential	The man **whose car broke down** called for help.
non-essential	My friend Sarah**, whose favourite colour is blue,** loves to paint.
non-essential	The dog**, whose tail wagged enthusiastically,** greeted us at the door.

essential	In the forest **where it's dark** is where you'll find the bears.
essential	Over there **where you see the bakery** is where you can buy the best sausage rolls.
non-essential	The party**, where everyone was dancing,** lasted until the early hours of the morning.
non-essential	The beach**, where the waves were crashing against the shore,** was a beautiful scene.

essential	The moment **when he heard the news** was full of sadness.
essential	The day **when she received her award** was the happiest of her life.
non-essential	The cat**, when it was hungry,** would meow loudly at the door.
non-essential	Before the party**, when no one was looking,** Aflie sneaked some sweets.

DICTATION SENTENCE ACTIVITIES

Sentence-level dictation is an important aspect of low-pressure sentence-level exposure. Teachers should dictate the sentences to the pupils, making it clear that the objective is to write a sentence, containing a relative clause.

When each sentence has been written by pupils, they should indicate the subject by circling it and the main verb by drawing a rectangle around it, before discussing with the teacher what the subject and verb might be and why. Discussion should also focus on the use of the relative pronoun, the clause and the comma, depending on whether the relative clause is **essential** or **non-essential**.

Embedded Essential Clauses (No Commas)

'The book **that I borrowed from the library** is due tomorrow.'

Teacher Explanation

In this sentence, the embedded relative clause 'that I borrowed from the library' is essential because it specifies which book is due tomorrow. Without this information, the sentence would lack clarity.

'The person **who stole my wallet** has been arrested.'

Teacher Explanation

Here, the embedded relative clause 'who stole my wallet' is essential because it identifies which person has been arrested. Without this information, the sentence would not specify who committed the theft.

'The movie **that we watched last night** was excellent.'

Here, the embedded relative clause 'that we watched last night' is essential because it specifies which movie was excellent. Without this information, the sentence would not convey the specific movie that the speaker is referring to.

Embedded Non-Essential Clauses (Use Commas)

'My friend**, who lives in London,** is coming to visit.'

Teacher Explanation

In this sentence, the embedded relative clause 'who lives in London' is non-essential because it provides additional information about the friend but is not necessary for identifying which friend is coming to visit.

'This restaurant**, where we had our first date,** has the best pizza in town.'

Teacher Explanation

Here, the embedded relative clause 'where we had our first date' is non-essential because it adds extra detail about the restaurant but is not crucial for identifying which restaurant has the best pizza in town.

'The cat**, which belongs to my neighbour,** often visits our garden.'

Teacher Explanation

In this sentence, the embedded relative clause 'which belongs to my neighbour' is non-essential because it provides additional information about the cat but is not necessary for identifying which cat often visits the garden.

COMPLETE THE SENTENCE

These activities require pupils to complete the sentences by adding the embedded relative clause. Pupils should be encouraged to make an active and conscious decision about whether or not the embedded relative clause being added is essential or non-essential. If it is essential, commas are not required. If the embedded relative clause is non-essential, commas are required.

Complete and punctuate the sentences with an embedded relative clause – 'who'.

Tip: If we expand the noun with an **essential** relative clause, then we don't need commas. If the extension is **non-essential,** then we will need to use commas.

I spent hours watching our puppy _____ play with his toys.
I tried to talk to Mum _____ about a problem.
She ran to her friend _____ to see if she was alright.

Complete and punctuate the sentences with an embedded relative clause – 'who'.

Tip: If we expand the noun with an **essential** relative clause, then we don't need commas. If the extension is **non-essential,** then we will need to use commas.

Marco visited the store _____ to buy some socks.
The bus _____ came around the corner.
She looked at the tower _____ in amazement.

Complete and punctuate the sentences with an embedded relative clause – 'who'.

Tip: If we expand the noun with an **essential** relative clause, then we don't need commas. If the extension is **non-essential,** then we will need to use commas.

My favourite meal _____ is fish and chips.
We got into the boat _____ to row across the river.
Mum stopped the car _____ to clean it.

Complete and punctuate the sentences with an embedded relative clause – 'who'.

Tip: If we expand the noun with an **essential** relative clause, then we don't need commas. If the extension is **non-essential,** then we will need to use commas.

I talked to the new boy at school _____ to make him feel welcome.
The woman _____ asked me for help.
All of the children _____ went to breakfast club.

Complete and punctuate the sentences with an embedded relative clause – 'who'.

Tip: If we expand the noun with an **essential** relative clause, then we don't need commas. If the extension is **non-essential,** then we will need to use commas.

Under the sofa _____ is dusty and dirty.
The back garden _____ is full of weeds.
In the distance _____ I can see lots of cows.

Complete and punctuate the sentences with an embedded relative clause – 'who'.

Tip: If we expand the noun with an **essential** relative clause, then we don't need commas. If the extension is **non-essential,** then we will need to use commas.

Just before bedtime _____ I like to sing songs.
After five minutes _____ the game continued.
While the dog was asleep _____ I finally relaxed.

COMPLETE THE SENTENCE

In the following activities, pupils need to focus on the noun that appears in the first part of the sentence, which we can see in **bold**. This noun will determine which pronoun pupils can potentially use. For example, if the noun is a name or a person, we would likely use the relative pronoun '**who**' to expand on the noun.

A further consideration is how we expand the sentence. If we expand the noun with an essential relative clause, then we don't need commas. If the extension is non-essential, then we will need to use commas. Try to encourage pupils to make a conscious and active decision here; ultimately, the sentence needs to read well.

I ran to **Freddy** _____ to ask if I could play.	
The **park** _____ was a great place to spend time.	
I was late for the **movie** _____ about superheroes.	
Just before **home time** _____ I collected my reading book.	
They ventured into the **jungle** _____ to find the gorillas.	
Miles brushed his **teeth** _____ then made his way downstairs.	
We listened to **Mrs Robson** _____ as she read the book.	
A **helicopter** _____ landed in the field.	
The local **park** _____ was deserted.	
We went to the **beach** _____ to look at the stars.	

The **book** _____ is due tomorrow.	
The **person** _____ has been arrested.	
The **car** _____ is a hybrid.	
The **movie** _____ was excellent.	
She chose the **person** _____ to speak during the interview.	
The **dog** _____ belongs to our neighbour.	
He remembers the **day** _____ he first learned to ride a bike.	
We'll go to the **park** _____ if the weather improves.	
She loves **time** _____ to relax and read a book.	
They recall the **period** _____ they travelled around Europe.	

The **restaurant** _____ has the best pizza in town.	
The **garden** _____ attracts many butterflies in the spring.	
The **painting** _____ sold for millions at auction.	
The **river** _____ flooded after heavy rainfall.	
The **computer** _____ was quickly fixed by the IT team.	
The **mountain** _____ is Mount Everest.	
The **writing** _____ received praise from the teacher.	
The **beach** _____ is a popular tourist destination.	
The **song** _____ was written by a local musician.	
The **event** _____ received lots of attention on the television.	

PRINTABLE PROMPTS

Print, cut and stick these sentence challenges into your pupils' books. Encourage pupils to create specific sentences that use relative embedded clauses. When they have written their sentences, the role the relative pronoun plays in each sentence, as well as the presence of the subject and the main verb in each clause and the use of punctuation, should be discussed with the pupils.

'who' – Relative Embedded Clause Challenge

Write three separate sentences using '**who**' as a relative pronoun, as part of an embedded relative clause.

Remember to think about whether the relative clause is **essential** (no commas) or **non-essential** (commas).

Each sentence should be punctuated correctly.

When you have finished each sentence, underline the relative pronoun, circle the subject and draw a rectangle around the verb in each clause.

'which' – Relative Embedded Clause Challenge

Write three separate sentences using '**which**' as a relative pronoun, as part of an embedded relative clause.

Remember to think about whether the relative clause is **essential** (no commas) or **non-essential** (commas).

Each sentence should be punctuated correctly.

When you have finished each sentence, underline the relative pronoun, circle the subject and draw a rectangle around the verb in each clause.

'that' – Relative Embedded Clause Challenge

Write three separate sentences using '**that**' as a relative pronoun, as part of an embedded relative clause.

Remember to think about whether the relative clause is **essential** (no commas) or **non-essential** (commas).

Each sentence should be punctuated correctly.

When you have finished each sentence, underline the relative pronoun, circle the subject and draw a rectangle around the verb in each clause.

'whose' – Relative Embedded Clause Challenge

Write three separate sentences using '**whose**' as a relative pronoun, as part of an embedded relative clause.

Remember to think about whether the relative clause is **essential** (no commas) or **non-essential** (commas).

Each sentence should be punctuated correctly.

When you have finished each sentence, underline the relative pronoun, circle the subject and draw a rectangle around the verb in each clause.

'where' – Relative Embedded Clause Challenge

Write three separate sentences using '**where**' as a relative pronoun, as part of an embedded relative clause.

Remember to think about whether the relative clause is **essential** (no commas) or **non-essential** (commas).

Each sentence should be punctuated correctly.

When you have finished each sentence, underline the relative pronoun, circle the subject and draw a rectangle around the verb in each clause.

'when' – Relative Embedded Clause Challenge

Write three separate sentences using '**when**' as a relative pronoun, as part of an embedded relative clause.

Remember to think about whether the relative clause is **essential** (no commas) or **non-essential** (commas).

Each sentence should be punctuated correctly.

When you have finished each sentence, underline the relative pronoun, circle the subject and draw a rectangle around the verb in each clause.

FORMATIVE ASSESSMENT PROMPTS

The resources found on the following pages can be used within a classroom or across the whole school to assess and track pupils' sentence-level skill. The prompts are relatively simple prompts, which ask pupils to write specific sentences that require them to demonstrate their knowledge of sentence types.

These can be completed easily and within a short time period of around five minutes. It is advisable to make this assessment extremely informal, to the point where the pupils see it as just another task, rather than an assessment. The information gleaned from the assessments will help teachers to better understand and track the depth and wealth of each pupil's sentence-level toolkit.

Sentence Toolkit Task

Relative Embedded Clause – 'who'

Task: You must write three sentences that contain a relative clause, using the relative pronoun '**who**'.

Leave a line between each sentence. Each sentence must be punctuated correctly.

Tip: Remember to think about the subject and the verb.

Sentence Toolkit Task

Relative Embedded Clause – 'which'

Task: You must write three sentences that contain a relative clause, using the relative pronoun '**which**'.

Leave a line between each sentence. Each sentence must be punctuated correctly.

Tip: Remember to think about the subject and the verb.

Sentence Toolkit Task

Relative Embedded Clause – 'that'

Task: You must write three sentences that contain a relative clause, using the relative pronoun '**that**'.

Leave a line between each sentence. Each sentence must be punctuated correctly.

Tip: Remember to think about the subject and the verb.

Sentence Toolkit Task

Relative Embedded Clause – 'whose'

Task: You must write three sentences that contain a relative clause, using the relative pronoun '**whose**'.

Leave a line between each sentence. Each sentence must be punctuated correctly.

Tip: Remember to think about the subject and the verb.

Sentence Toolkit Task

Relative Embedded Clause – 'where'

Task: You must write three sentences that contain a relative clause, using the relative pronoun '**where**'.

Leave a line between each sentence. Each sentence must be punctuated correctly.

Tip: Remember to think about the subject and the verb.

Sentence Toolkit Task

Relative Embedded Clause – 'when'

Task: You must write three sentences that contain a relative clause, using the relative pronoun '**when**'.

Leave a line between each sentence. Each sentence must be punctuated correctly.

Tip: Remember to think about the subject and the verb.

Sentence Ninja © Andrew Jennings, 2025

SCAFFOLDED FORMATIVE ASSESSMENT PROMPTS

These scaffolded resources provide additional support and advice for pupils.

Sentence Toolkit Task
Embedded Relative Clause – 'who'

Task: You must write three sentences that contain an embedded relative clause, using the relative pronoun **'who'**.

Leave a line between each sentence. Each sentence must be punctuated correctly.

Tip: Remember to think about the subject and the verb.

Tip: If you are struggling for inspiration, think about a setting, character or situation from a book you are reading.

Tip: If the relative clause is **essential**, there should <u>not</u> be commas. If the clause is **non-essential**, there <u>should</u> be commas.

Sentence Toolkit Task
Embedded Relative Clause – 'which'

Task: You must write three sentences that contain an embedded relative clause, using the relative pronoun **'which'**.

Leave a line between each sentence. Each sentence must be punctuated correctly.

Tip: Remember to think about the subject and the verb.

Tip: If you are struggling for inspiration, think about a setting, character or situation from a book you are reading.

Tip: If the relative clause is **essential**, there should <u>not</u> be commas. If the clause is **non-essential**, there <u>should</u> be commas.

Sentence Toolkit Task
Embedded Relative Clause – 'that'

Task: You must write three sentences that contain an embedded relative clause, using the relative pronoun **'that'**.

Leave a line between each sentence. Each sentence must be punctuated correctly.

Tip: Remember to think about the subject and the verb.

Tip: If you are struggling for inspiration, think about a setting, character or situation from a book you are reading.

Tip: If the relative clause is **essential**, there should <u>not</u> be commas. If the clause is **non-essential**, there <u>should</u> be commas.

Sentence Toolkit Task
Embedded Relative Clause – 'whose'

Task: You must write three sentences that contain an embedded relative clause, using the relative pronoun **'whose'**.

Leave a line between each sentence. Each sentence must be punctuated correctly.

Tip: Remember to think about the subject and the verb.

Tip: If you are struggling for inspiration, think about a setting, character or situation from a book you are reading.

Tip: If the relative clause is **essential**, there should <u>not</u> be commas. If the clause is **non-essential**, there <u>should</u> be commas.

Sentence Toolkit Task
Embedded Relative Clause – 'where'

Task: You must write three sentences that contain an embedded relative clause, using the relative pronoun **'where'**.

Leave a line between each sentence. Each sentence must be punctuated correctly.

Tip: Remember to think about the subject and the verb.

Tip: If you are struggling for inspiration, think about a setting, character or situation from a book you are reading.

Tip: If the relative clause is **essential**, there should <u>not</u> be commas. If the clause is **non-essential**, there <u>should</u> be commas.

Sentence Toolkit Task
Embedded Relative Clause – 'when'

Task: You must write three sentences that contain an embedded relative clause, using the relative pronoun **'when'**.

Leave a line between each sentence. Each sentence must be punctuated correctly.

Tip: Remember to think about the subject and the verb.

Tip: If you are struggling for inspiration, think about a setting, character or situation from a book you are reading.

Tip: If the relative clause is **essential**, there should <u>not</u> be commas. If the clause is **non-essential**, there <u>should</u> be commas.

VARIED ASSESSMENT PROMPTS

Varied Assessment Prompts provide a range of assessment activities with varied conjunction and sentence-level expectations. These prompts are ideal for you to use to accurately assess what sentence-level skills your pupils can independently apply.

Sentence Toolkit Task	
Embedded Relative Clauses – 'who', 'which', 'that'	
Task: You must write three sentences that contain an embedded relative clause. Each sentence should use one of the following relative pronouns: **'who'**, **'which'** and **'that'**. Leave a line between each sentence. Remember to punctuate each sentence.	
Tip: If the relative clause is **essential**, there should **not** be commas. If the clause is **non-essential**, there **should** be commas.	
Sentence Checklist (Tick off each sentence as you write.)	who ☐ which ☐ that ☐
Challenge: Once you have completed each sentence, circle the subject and draw a rectangle around the verb in each clause.	

Sentence Toolkit Task	
Embedded Relative Clauses – 'whose', 'where', 'when'	
Task: You must write three sentences that contain an embedded relative clause. Each sentence should use one of the following relative pronouns: **'whose'**, **'where'** and **'when'**. Leave a line between each sentence. Remember to punctuate each sentence.	
Tip: If the relative clause is **essential**, there should **not** be commas. If the clause is **non-essential**, there **should** be commas.	
Sentence Checklist (Tick off each sentence as you write.)	whose ☐ where ☐ when ☐
Challenge: Once you have completed each sentence, circle the subject and draw a rectangle around the verb in each clause.	

Sentence Toolkit Task	
Embedded Relative Clauses – 'which', 'that', 'where'	
Task: You must write three sentences that contain an embedded relative clause. Each sentence should use one of the following relative pronouns: **'which'**, **'that'** and **'where'**. Leave a line between each sentence. Remember to punctuate each sentence.	
Tip: If the relative clause is **essential**, there should **not** be commas. If the clause is **non-essential**, there **should** be commas.	
Sentence Checklist (Tick off each sentence as you write.)	which ☐ that ☐ where ☐
Challenge: Once you have completed each sentence, circle the subject and draw a rectangle around the verb in each clause.	

Sentence Toolkit Task	
Embedded Relative Clauses – 'who', 'which', 'that', 'whose', 'where', 'when'	
Task: You must write **six** different sentences that use an embedded relative clause beginning with a relative pronoun. Each sentence should use one of the **six** relative pronouns: **'who'**, **'which'**, **'that'**, **'whose'**, **'where'** and **'when'**. Leave a line between each sentence. Remember to punctuate each sentence.	
Tip: If the relative clause is **essential**, there should **not** be commas. If the clause is **non-essential**, there **should** be commas.	
Sentence Checklist (Tick off each sentence as you write.)	who ☐ which ☐ that ☐ whose ☐ where ☐ when ☐
Challenge: Once you have completed each sentence, circle the subject and draw a rectangle around the verb in each clause.	

PACE MILESTONES

PACE milestones are periods of reflection encompassed by the PACE acronym. They enable us to dive deeper into the previous terms' content and skills to ensure that the curriculum doesn't just superficially continue to move on without the depth that we really require. This period also allows for additional support for those children who require it.

But what is PACE and what does it stand for?

Practise: Engage in regular exercises or activities to build proficiency in writing basic sentences in a variety of structures.

Apply: Apply newly learned sentences from the previous term(s) in various contexts, genres and micro-activities.

Consolidate: Consolidate learning through teacher modelling, revision and integration of newly acquired skills.

Enable: Empower the child to become more confident in their writing abilities and foster a sense of independence.

PACE MILESTONE 1 – SIMPLE SENTENCES

PACE Milestone 1 focuses solely on the consolidation of simple sentences and the use of 'and' to build compound sentences.

They are the first of a series of PACE Milestones designed to ensure that pupils have secure knowledge of the building blocks of sentence structure and are provided opportunities to practise and apply this understanding. During this period, teachers should be using the PACE activities to get a sound and detailed understanding of pupil sentence-level competence via informal assessment. Teachers should quickly look to intervene with pupils who require additional support to secure their understanding.

PACE Milestone 1

Simple Sentence Structure

Context: A knight called Sir Puresword needs to defeat an evil dragon to save the village of Ragton.

Task: Write up to 5 simple sentences that relate to the context above.

Practise: Writing a simple sentence that contains a subject and a verb.

- Leave a line between each sentence.
- Sentences must be punctuated correctly.
- Circle the subject and draw a rectangle around the verb.

Think about: what the knight or the dragon might do.

PACE Milestone 1

Simple Sentence Structure

Context: Your local pond is full of litter and local people are working together to clean it up.

Task: Write up to 5 simple sentences that relate to the context above.

Practise: Writing a simple sentence that contains a subject and a verb.

- Leave a line between each sentence.
- Sentences must be punctuated correctly.
- Circle the subject and draw a rectangle around the verb.

Think about: what sort of litter is in the pond and what people are using to clean it up.

PACE Milestone 1

Simple Sentence Structure

Context: A volcano has erupted in Iceland. Lava is flowing towards the local town. Local people are worried.

Task: Write up to 5 simple sentences that relate to the context above.

Practise: Writing a simple sentence that contains a subject and a verb.

- Leave a line between each sentence.
- Sentences must be punctuated correctly.
- Circle the subject and draw a rectangle around the verb.

Think about: how the volcano erupted, what the people are doing and what the lava is doing.

PACE Milestone 1

Simple Sentence Structure

Context: A witch is making a potion in her cauldron, while her cat watches her. The witch is using lots of strange ingredients.

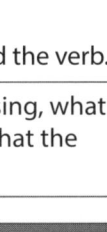

Task: Write up to 5 simple sentences that relate to the context above.

Practise: Writing a simple sentence that contains a subject and a verb.

- Leave a line between each sentence.
- Sentences must be punctuated correctly.
- Circle the subject and draw a rectangle around the verb.

Think about: what ingredients the witch is using, what she will create with her finished potion and what the cat is doing.

PACE Milestone 1

Simple Sentence Structure

Context: Children are tidying up your classroom before home time.

Task: Write up to 5 simple sentences that relate to the context above.

Practise: Writing a simple sentence that contains a subject and a verb.

- Leave a line between each sentence.
- Sentences must be punctuated correctly.
- Circle the subject and draw a rectangle around the verb.

Think about: what the children are tidying up and how they feel.

PACE Milestone 1

Simple Sentence Structure

Context: It's playtime on the school playground. What do you see?

Task: Write up to 5 simple sentences that relate to the context above.

Practise: Writing a simple sentence that contains a subject and a verb.

- Leave a line between each sentence.
- Sentences must be punctuated correctly.
- Circle the subject and draw a rectangle around the verb.

Think about: what is happening in the playground, who else is on the playground and how you feel.

Sentence Ninja © Andrew Jennings, 2025

PACE MILESTONE 1 – COMPOUND SENTENCES (AND)

PACE Milestone 1
Compound Sentence Structure (and)

Context: It's dinner time and Alice has been asked to set the table ready for everyone to eat.

Task: Write 3 compound sentences using the coordinating conjunction '**and**' that relate to the context above.

Practise: Writing a compound sentence using '**and**' as a coordinating conjunction.

- Leave a line between each sentence.
- Sentences must be punctuated correctly.
- Circle the subject and draw a rectangle around the verb.

Think about: what Alice might need to do, what equipment she might use and where she is.

Remember: '**and**' joins two clauses together.

PACE Milestone 1
Compound Sentence Structure (and)

Context: Ben is at the beach with his family. They spend the whole day playing games, building sandcastles and having fun.

Task: Write 3 compound sentences using the coordinating conjunction '**and**' that relate to the context above.

Practise: Writing a compound sentence using '**and**' as a coordinating conjunction.

- Leave a line between each sentence.
- Sentences must be punctuated correctly.
- Circle the subject and draw a rectangle around the verb.

Think about: the things Ben might do, who he is with and what games they might play. Think about things you do at the beach.

Remember: '**and**' joins two clauses together.

PACE Milestone 1
Compound Sentence Structure (and)

Context: Rocco is an explorer, making her way through the dangerous jungle. It's full of dangerous animals. She is looking for an ancient temple but she is lost.

Task: Write 3 compound sentences using the coordinating conjunction '**and**' that relate to the context above.

Practise: Writing a compound sentence using '**and**' as a coordinating conjunction.

- Leave a line between each sentence.
- Sentences must be punctuated correctly.
- Circle the subject and draw a rectangle around the verb.

Think about: what animals Rocco might see or encounter and how they would move. Think about what makes a jungle dangerous.

Remember: '**and**' joins two clauses together.

PACE Milestone 1
Compound Sentence Structure (and)

Context: Robbie is on her way to school with her brother, Mark. They are walking. It's hot. They stop at the shop for a drink. They see their uncle in the shop.

Task: Write 3 compound sentences using the coordinating conjunction '**and**' that relate to the context above.

Practise: Writing a compound sentence using '**and**' as a coordinating conjunction.

- Leave a line between each sentence.
- Sentences must be punctuated correctly.
- Circle the subject and draw a rectangle around the verb.

Think about: what drinks Robbie and Mark might buy in the shop and if they were late or on time for school. Think about what their uncle was buying in the shop.

Remember: '**and**' joins two clauses together.

PACE MILESTONE 2 – COMPOUND SENTENCES

PACE Milestone 2 covers compound sentences and complex sentences. These tasks allow teachers to informally assess pupils and to intervene where necessary, with active modelling and sentence-level instruction. This is the '**C**onsolidation and **E**nable' element of PACE.

PACE Milestone 2
Compound Sentence Structure (and)

Context: Think about lessons and activities at school. Think about tasks or activities you might do together or one after another.

Task: Write 3 compound sentences using the coordinating conjunction '**and**' that relate to the context above.

Practise: Writing a compound sentence using '**and**' as a coordinating conjunction.
- Leave a line between each sentence.
- Sentences must be punctuated correctly.
- Circle the subject and draw a rectangle around the verb in each clause.

Think about: the subjects you are taught, such as English, history, art and PE. Think about what you do in these subjects and what equipment you use.

Remember: '**and**' joins two clauses together.

PACE Milestone 2
Compound Sentence Structure (and)

Context: You are on safari. Looking through your binoculars, you see different animals. Tell us about the animals you see and describe what they are doing.

Task: Write 3 compound sentences using the coordinating conjunction '**and**' that relate to the context above.

Practise: Writing a compound sentence using '**and**' as a coordinating conjunction.
- Leave a line between each sentence.
- Sentences must be punctuated correctly.
- Circle the subject and draw a rectangle around the verb in each clause.

Think about: the animals you might see on a safari. Think about how they move and what they would normally do.

Remember: '**and**' joins two clauses together.

PACE Milestone 2
Compound Sentence Structure (but)

Context: Think about the story of the three little pigs. Consider why the pigs built their houses, and think about the problems that occurred because of the materials they chose.

Task: Write 3 compound sentences using the coordinating conjunction '**but**' that relate to the context above.

Practise: Writing a compound sentence using '**but**' as a coordinating conjunction.
- Leave a line between each sentence.
- Sentences must be punctuated correctly.
- Circle the subject and draw a rectangle around the verb in each clause.

Think about: how the pigs felt about their houses and why the wolf decided to blow the houses down.

Remember: '**but**' contrasts two clauses.

PACE Milestone 2
Compound Sentence Structure (but)

Context: Think about the story of Jack and the Beanstalk, including Jack's mum, the cow, the magic beans, the beanstalk, the goose that lays golden eggs and the giant.

Task: Write 3 compound sentences using the coordinating conjunction '**but**' that relate to the context above.

Practise: Writing a compound sentence using '**but**' as a coordinating conjunction.
- Leave a line between each sentence.
- Sentences must be punctuated correctly.
- Circle the subject and draw a rectangle around the verb in each clause.

Think about: why Jack goes up the beanstalk and what he takes. Think about how the giant feels and if the situation is dangerous.

Remember: '**but**' contrasts two clauses.

PACE Milestone 2
Compound Sentence Structure (so)

Context: Think about a time when you were at home or school when you did something to help a parent, teacher or friend. What did you do and why?

Task: Write 3 compound sentences using the coordinating conjunction '**so**' that relate to the context above.

Practise: Writing a compound sentence using '**so**' as a coordinating conjunction.
- Leave a line between each sentence.
- Sentences must be punctuated correctly.
- Circle the subject and draw a rectangle around the verb in each clause.

Think about: what kind things you might have done before to be helpful. Consider why you were helpful and what you wanted to happen.

Remember: '**so**' is used to show the result or the 'why?' of the first clause.

PACE Milestone 2
Compound Sentence Structure (so)

Context: Think about books you have read or films you have watched. What things have the main characters done and why?

Task: Write 3 compound sentences using the coordinating conjunction '**so**' that relate to the context above.

Practise: Writing a compound sentence using '**so**' as a coordinating conjunction.
- Leave a line between each sentence.
- Sentences must be punctuated correctly.
- Circle the subject and draw a rectangle around the verb in each clause.

Think about: the books that you have you read. Think about the characters and what you remember them doing. Consider why they did those things.

Remember: '**so**' is used to show the result or the 'why?' of the first clause.

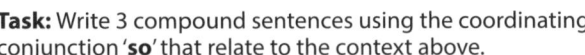

PACE MILESTONE 2 – COMPOUND SENTENCES (AND, BUT, SO)

These PACE activities provide opportunities for pupils to practise and apply their understanding of multiple coordinating conjunctions and how they can be used to form compound sentences. Teachers can use these tasks to get an accurate understanding of pupil sentence-level competence.

PACE Milestone 2
Compound Sentence Structure ('and', 'but', 'so')

Context: You need to cross a river. You are with a friend and they are worried. There is a small rowing boat that you can use to cross the river. The water is moving quite fast. It's starting to get dark.

Task: Write 3 different compound sentences using the coordinating conjunctions '**and**', '**but**', '**so**' that relate to the context above.

Practise: Writing a compound sentence using '**and**', '**but**', '**so**' as a coordinating conjunction.

- Leave a line between each sentence.
- Sentences must be punctuated correctly.

Sentence Checklist (Tick off each sentence as you write.)   and ☐   but ☐   so ☐

Challenge: Once you have completed each sentence, circle the subject and draw a rectangle around the verb in each clause.

PACE Milestone 2
Compound Sentence Structure ('and', 'but', 'so')

Context: It's the Great Fire of London. You are in the street and you can see the fire starting to spread from one house to the next. It's spreading so fast!

Task: Write 3 different compound sentences using the coordinating conjunctions '**and**', '**but**', '**so**' that relate to the context above.

Practise: Writing a compound sentence using '**and**', '**but**', '**so**' as a coordinating conjunction.

- Leave a line between each sentence.
- Sentences must be punctuated correctly.

Sentence Checklist (Tick off each sentence as you write.)   and ☐   but ☐   so ☐

Challenge: Once you have completed each sentence, circle the subject and draw a rectangle around the verb in each clause.

PACE Milestone 2
Compound Sentence Structure ('and', 'but', 'so')

Context: You find yourself in the middle of a spooky graveyard. You don't know how you got there. There are lots of sounds and movements around you. You can see shadows. You are a little bit scared.

Task: Write 3 different compound sentences using the coordinating conjunctions '**and**', '**but**', '**so**' that relate to the context above.

Practise: Writing a compound sentence using '**and**', '**but**', '**so**' as a coordinating conjunction.

- Leave a line between each sentence.
- Sentences must be punctuated correctly.

Sentence Checklist (Tick off each sentence as you write.)   and ☐   but ☐   so ☐

Challenge: Once you have completed each sentence, circle the subject and draw a rectangle around the verb in each clause.

PACE MILESTONE 2 – COMPLEX SENTENCES (WHEN, IF, BECAUSE)

PACE Milestone 2
Compound Sentence Structure (when)

Context: Freddie is fishing. He's sitting by the side of a river. It's sunny and he's very happy.

Task: Write 3 complex sentences using the subordinating conjunction '**when**' that relate to the context above.

Practise: Writing a complex sentence using '**when**' as a subordinating conjunction.
- Leave a line between each sentence.
- Sentences must be punctuated correctly.
- Circle the subject and draw a rectangle around the verb in each clause.

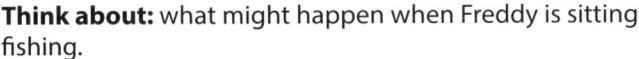

Think about: what might happen when Freddy is sitting fishing.

Remember: '**when**' means 'at that time'.

PACE Milestone 2
Complex Sentence Structure (when)

Context: Samiha is reading her book in her bedroom. It's quiet and she's lost in the story.

Task: Write 3 complex sentences using the subordinating conjunction '**when**' that relate to the context above.

Practise: Writing a complex sentence using '**when**' as a subordinating conjunction.
- Leave a line between each sentence.
- Sentences must be punctuated correctly.
- Circle the subject and draw a rectangle around the verb in each clause.

Think about: what might happen when Samiha is reading her book.

Remember: '**when**' means 'at that time'.

PACE Milestone 2
Compound Sentence Structure (if)

Context: A fox is scavenging because it's hungry. The fox can't find any food. It decides to continue looking near houses.

Task: Write 3 complex sentences using the subordinating conjunction '**if**' that relate to the context above.

Practise: Writing a complex sentence using '**if**' as a subordinating conjunction.
- Leave a line between each sentence.
- Sentences must be punctuated correctly.
- Circle the subject and draw a rectangle around the verb in each clause.

Think about: what the fox finding food depends on.

Remember: '**if**' shows a condition that something else depends on.

PACE Milestone 2
Complex Sentence Structure (if)

Context: Mia is planning her diary for the summer holidays and is thinking about all of the things she'd like to be able to do.

Task: Write 3 complex sentences using the subordinating conjunction '**if**' that relate to the context above.

Practise: Writing a complex sentence using '**if**' as a subordinating conjunction.
- Leave a line between each sentence.
- Sentences must be punctuated correctly.
- Circle the subject and draw a rectangle around the verb in each clause.

Think about: all of the things that Mia would like to do.

Remember: '**if**' shows a condition that something else depends on.

PACE Milestone 2
Compound Sentence Structure (because)

Context: A firefighter is in the fire station. They are preparing all of the equipment they need for the day, making sure everything is ready and working.

Task: Write 3 complex sentences using the subordinating conjunction '**because**' that relate to the context above.

Practise: Writing a complex sentence using '**because**' as a subordinating conjunction.
- Leave a line between each sentence.
- Sentences must be punctuated correctly.
- Circle the subject and draw a rectangle around the verb in each clause.

Think about: the equipment this job requires and the reasons that certain equipment is required.

Remember: '**because**' explains a reason or cause.

PACE Milestone 2
Complex Sentence Structure (because)

Context: Three children want to visit three different locations, for three different reasons. Who are the children? What do they want to do and why?

Task: Write 3 complex sentences using the subordinating conjunction '**because**' that relate to the context above.

Practise: Writing a complex sentence using '**because**' as a subordinating conjunction.
- Leave a line between each sentence.
- Sentences must be punctuated correctly.
- Circle the subject and draw a rectangle around the verb in each clause.

Think about: the places the children might like to visit and why.

Remember: '**because**' explains a reason or cause.

PACE MILESTONE 2 – COMPLEX SENTENCES (WHEN, IF, BECAUSE)

These PACE activities provide opportunities for pupils to practise and apply their understanding of multiple subordinating conjunctions and how they can be used to form complex sentences. Teachers can use these tasks to get an accurate understanding of pupil sentence-level competence.

PACE Milestone 2

Complex Sentence Structure ('when', 'if', 'because')

Context: Think about your school. What are some of the things that you think might improve your school for all of the pupils? Think about why these things might make your school better.

Task: Write 3 different complex sentences using the subordinating conjunctions '**when**', '**if**', '**because**' that relate to the context above.

Practise: Writing a complex sentence using '**when**', '**if**', '**because**' as a subordinating conjunction.

Clauses: Think about varying the position of your main and subordinate clauses.

• Leave a line between each sentence.
• Sentences must be punctuated correctly.

Sentence Checklist (Tick off each sentence as you write.)   when ☐   if ☐   because ☐

Challenge: Once you have completed each sentence, circle the subject and draw a rectangle around the verb in each clause.

PACE Milestone 2

Complex Sentence Structure ('when', 'if', 'because')

Context: A polar bear is hunting in the Arctic. There is a blizzard and it's -20 degrees Celsius.

Task: Write 3 different complex sentences using the subordinating conjunctions '**when**', '**if**', '**because**' that relate to the context above.

Practise: Writing a complex sentence using '**when**', '**if**', '**because**' as a subordinating conjunction.

Clauses: Think about varying the position of your main and subordinate clauses.

• Leave a line between each sentence.
• Sentences must be punctuated correctly.

Sentence Checklist (Tick off each sentence as you write.)   when ☐   if ☐   because ☐

Challenge: Once you have completed each sentence, circle the subject and draw a rectangle around the verb in each clause.

PACE Milestone 2

Complex Sentence Structure ('when', 'if', 'because')

Context: A famous actor is visiting your school to film a scene for a movie. There's a buzz and everyone is very excited, even the teachers.

Task: Write 3 different complex sentences using the subordinating conjunctions '**when**', '**if**', '**because**' that relate to the context above.

Practise: Writing a complex sentence using '**when**', '**if**', '**because**' as a subordinating conjunction.

Clauses: Think about varying the position of your main and subordinate clauses.

• Leave a line between each sentence.
• Sentences must be punctuated correctly.

Sentence Checklist (Tick off each sentence as you write.)   when ☐   if ☐   because ☐

Challenge: Once you have completed each sentence, circle the subject and draw a rectangle around the verb in each clause.

PACE MILESTONE 2 – COMPOUND SENTENCES (AND, BUT, SO) AND COMPLEX SENTENCES (WHEN, IF, BECAUSE)

PACE Milestone 2
Compound and Complex Sentence Structures
('and', 'but', 'so' and 'when', 'if', 'because')

Context: It's lunchtime and children are everywhere. Some children are eating hot meals, others are eating packed lunches. A few children are full of energy and eager to get outside whereas other children are tired. Some children are sad and some are being noisy. Think about the different children and their motivations.

Task: Write 6 different sentences using the coordinating conjunctions '**and**', '**but**', '**so**' and the subordinating conjunctions '**when**', '**if**', '**because**' that relate to the context above.

Start with the conjunctions you feel most confident using.

Clauses: Think about varying the position of your main and subordinate clauses in your complex sentences.

Sentence Checklist (Tick off each sentence as you write.)	and ☐ but ☐ so ☐ when ☐ if ☐ because ☐

Challenge: Once you have completed each sentence, circle the subject and draw a rectangle around the verb in each clause.

PACE Milestone 2
Compound and Complex Sentence Structures
('and', 'but', 'so' and 'when', 'if', 'because')

Context: There are many families and children in the busy playground. It's sunny and a little bit windy too. There are many pieces of equipment that children are playing on. Not all the parents are paying attention.

Task: Write 6 different sentences using the coordinating conjunctions '**and**', '**but**', '**so**' and the subordinating conjunctions '**when**', '**if**', '**because**' that relate to the context above.

Start with the conjunctions you feel most confident using.

Clauses: Think about varying the position of your main and subordinate clauses in your complex sentences.

Sentence Checklist (Tick off each sentence as you write.)	and ☐ but ☐ so ☐ when ☐ if ☐ because ☐

Challenge: Once you have completed each sentence, circle the subject and draw a rectangle around the verb in each clause.

PACE Milestone 2
Compound and Complex Sentence Structures
('and', 'but', 'so' and 'when', 'if', 'because')

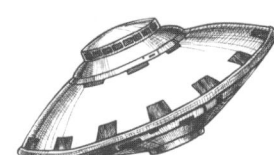

Context: An alien spaceship has landed on the local field. There is lots of smoke. Some people are gathered around the ship and are excited. Other people are very worried and some have even left town. The police are there and all of the local schools have been closed.

Task: Write 6 different sentences using the coordinating conjunctions '**and**', '**but**', '**so**' and the subordinating conjunctions '**when**', '**if**', '**because**' that relate to the context above.

Start with the conjunctions you feel most confident using.

Clauses: Think about varying the position of your main and subordinate clauses in your complex sentences.

Sentence Checklist (Tick off each sentence as you write.)	and ☐ but ☐ so ☐ when ☐ if ☐ because ☐

Challenge: Once you have completed each sentence, circle the subject and draw a rectangle around the verb in each clause.

PACE MILESTONE 3 – COMPOUND SENTENCES (YET, OR, NOR/FOR)

PACE Milestone 3 covers compound sentences and complex sentences. These tasks allow teachers to informally assess pupils and to intervene where necessary, with active modelling and sentence-level instruction. This is the '**C**onsolidation and **E**nable' element of PACE.

PACE Milestone 3
Compound Sentence Structure (yet)

Context: Alex is in a shop and really wants to buy a certain item. It's quite expensive. She has saved a lot of money to buy the item.

Task: Write 3 compound sentences using the coordinating conjunction '**yet**' that relate to the context above.

Practise: Writing a compound sentence using '**yet**' as a coordinating conjunction.
- Leave a line between each sentence.
- Sentences must be punctuated correctly.
- Circle the subject and draw a rectangle around the verb in each clause.

Think about: what the item is, what might be going through her head and how long she has saved for.

Remember: '**yet**' contrasts two clauses (like 'but').

PACE Milestone 3
Compound Sentence Structure (yet)

Context: Courtney is excited to go on the school residential. The teacher asked the pupils to bring lots of items to do the activities (climbing, kayaking, etc.). All of a sudden Courtney realises she hasn't remembered everything.

Task: Write 3 compound sentences using the coordinating conjunction '**yet**' that relate to the context above.

Practise: Writing a compound sentence using '**yet**' as a coordinating conjunction.
- Leave a line between each sentence.
- Sentences must be punctuated correctly.
- Circle the subject and draw a rectangle around the verb in each clause.

Think about: what Courtney has forgotten and what she now won't be able to do.

Remember: '**yet**' contrasts two clauses (like 'but').

PACE Milestone 3
Compound Sentence Structure (or)

Context: Morgan is at her favourite book store. She has a choice between two books. She reads the blurb on the back cover of each book.

Task: Write 3 compound sentences using the coordinating conjunction '**or**' that relate to the context above.

Practise: Writing a compound sentence using '**or**' as a coordinating conjunction.
- Leave a line between each sentence.
- Sentences must be punctuated correctly.
- Circle the subject and draw a rectangle around the verb in each clause.

Think about: what each book is about and what Morgan likes about each book.

Remember: '**or**' joins two clauses to show two options, alternatives or possibilities.

PACE Milestone 3
Compound Sentence Structure (or)

Context: Jenny needs to get to her friend's house. She doesn't know which mode of transport to take – bicycle, bus, car, taxi or by foot.

Task: Write 3 compound sentences using the coordinating conjunction '**or**' that relate to the context above.

Practise: Writing a compound sentence using '**or**' as a coordinating conjunction.
- Leave a line between each sentence.
- Sentences must be punctuated correctly.
- Circle the subject and draw a rectangle around the verb in each clause.

Think about: why Jenny might use a certain mode of transport.

Remember: '**or**' joins two clauses to show two options, alternatives or possibilities.

PACE Milestone
Compound Sentence Structure (nor/for)

Context: James is having a bad day. He hasn't remembered his PE kit. He's also forgotten other things that are happening today.

Task: Write 3 compound sentences using the coordinating conjunction '**nor/for**' that relate to the context above.

Practise: Writing a compound sentence using '**nor/for**' as a coordinating conjunction.
- Leave a line between each sentence.
- Sentences must be punctuated correctly.
- Circle the subject and draw a rectangle around the verb in each clause.

Think about: what else has James not done? What has he forgotten about today? How does he feel about it?

PACE Milestone 3
Compound Sentence Structure (nor/for)

Context: Sara isn't having a party for her birthday because of the weather. Think about what else might not be going well or might now not happen.

Task: Write 3 compound sentences using the coordinating conjunction '**nor/for**' that relate to the context above.

Practise: Writing a compound sentence using '**nor/for**' as a coordinating conjunction.
- Leave a line between each sentence.
- Sentences must be punctuated correctly.
- Circle the subject and draw a rectangle around the verb in each clause.

Think about: how Sara might be feeling. Consider who was going to the party and if it will be rearranged.

PACE MILESTONE 3 – COMPOUND SENTENCES (OR, YET, NOR/FOR)

PACE Milestone 3
Compound Sentence Structure ('or', 'yet', 'nor'/'for')

Context: Think about a person who is jumping out of an aeroplane for charity. They are sitting in the door of the plane, high up in the sky. How are the feeling? What are they thinking? The pilot shouts, 'Go, go, go!'

Task: Write 3 different compound sentences using the coordinating conjunctions **'or'**, **'yet'**, **'nor'**/**'for'** that relate to the context above.

Practise: Writing a compound sentence using **'or'**, **'yet'**, **'nor'**/**'for'** as a coordinating conjunction.

- Leave a line between each sentence.
- Sentences must be punctuated correctly.

Sentence Checklist (Tick off each sentence as you write.)   or ☐   yet ☐   nor/for ☐

Challenge: Once you have completed each sentence, circle the subject and draw a rectangle around the verb in each clause.

PACE Milestone 3
Compound Sentence Structure ('or', 'yet', 'nor'/'for')

Context: It's the summer holidays. The weather is amazing and everyone is so hot. Everyone is also super bored, as there is nothing to do. Amy is in her garden, bored, trying to think of something to do.

Task: Write 3 different compound sentences using the coordinating conjunctions **'or'**, **'yet'**, **'nor'**/**'for'** that relate to the context above.

Practise: Writing a compound sentence using **'or'**, **'yet'**, **'nor'**/**'for'** as a coordinating conjunction.

- Leave a line between each sentence.
- Sentences must be punctuated correctly.

Sentence Checklist (Tick off each sentence as you write.)   or ☐   yet ☐   nor/for ☐

Challenge: Once you have completed each sentence, circle the subject and draw a rectangle around the verb in each clause.

PACE Milestone 3
Compound Sentence Structure ('or', 'yet', 'nor'/'for')

Context: Mark's football team is getting beaten 4–0 at half time. Some of the players have given up, but the coach thinks they can still win the game. Mark isn't sure as he's already very tired.

Task: Write 3 different compound sentences using the coordinating conjunctions **'or'**, **'yet'**, **'nor'**/**'for'** that relate to the context above.

Practise: Writing a compound sentence using **'or'**, **'yet'**, **'nor'**/**'for'** as a coordinating conjunction.

- Leave a line between each sentence.
- Sentences must be punctuated correctly.

Sentence Checklist (Tick off each sentence as you write.)   or ☐   yet ☐   nor/for ☐

Challenge: Once you have completed each sentence, circle the subject and draw a rectangle around the verb in each clause.

PACE MILESTONE 3 – COMPLEX SENTENCES (ALTHOUGH, WHILE, UNLESS)

PACE Milestone 3
Compound Sentence Structure (although)

Context: Julie is at a theme park. She loves rides, but the three friends she is with don't like the same rides and attractions.

Task: Write 3 complex sentences using the subordinating conjunction '**although**' that relate to the context above.

Practise: Writing a complex sentence using '**although**' as a subordinating conjunction.
- Leave a line between each sentence.
- Sentences must be punctuated correctly.
- Circle the subject and draw a rectangle around the verb in each clause.

Think about: what Julie likes and what her friends do and don't like. Try not to use 'because'.

Remember: '**although**' connects contrasting or contradictory information.

PACE Milestone 3
Complex Sentence Structure (although)

Context: Pedro is at a car boot sale, looking for bargains. He speaks to lots of people to try and buy items. Pedro loves haggling.

Task: Write 3 complex sentences using the subordinating conjunction '**although**' that relate to the context above.

Practise: Writing a complex sentence using '**although**' as a subordinating conjunction.
- Leave a line between each sentence.
- Sentences must be punctuated correctly.
- Circle the subject and draw a rectangle around the verb in each clause.

Think about: what Pedro is trying to buy. Think about the prices he pays for items and if he buys everything he wants. Are some things broken or too expensive?

Remember: '**although**' connects contrasting or contradictory information.

PACE Milestone 3
Compound Sentence Structure (while)

Context: Two children are playing together. They are both doing different things at the same time.

Task: Write 3 complex sentences using the subordinating conjunction '**while**' that relate to the context above.

Practise: Writing a complex sentence using '**while**' as a subordinating conjunction.
- Leave a line between each sentence.
- Sentences must be punctuated correctly.
- Circle the subject and draw a rectangle around the verb in each clause.

Think about: the different things that the children are doing.

Remember: '**while**' shows an action or event, as another is happening.

PACE Milestone 3
Complex Sentence Structure (while)

Context: Children are in an art lesson where they are building models, painting and drawing. The teacher is moving around and helping the children.

Task: Write 3 complex sentences using the subordinating conjunction '**while**' that relate to the context above.

Practise: Writing a complex sentence using '**while**' as a subordinating conjunction.
- Leave a line between each sentence.
- Sentences must be punctuated correctly.
- Circle the subject and draw a rectangle around the verb in each clause.

Think about: the different things that children in the classroom might be doing.

Remember: '**while**' shows an action or event, as another is happening.

PACE Milestone 3
Compound Sentence Structure (unless)

Context: Think about things you have wanted to do in the past, where you have needed to do another thing for the first to happen.

Task: Write 3 complex sentences using the subordinating conjunction '**unless**' that relate to the context above.

Practise: Writing a complex sentence using '**unless**' as a subordinating conjunction.
- Leave a line between each sentence.
- Sentences must be punctuated correctly.
- Circle the subject and draw a rectangle around the verb in each clause.

Think about: the sorts of things you wanted to do, that could only happen if you did something else first.

Remember: '**unless**' shows that something will or will not happen '**unless**' another action happens or condition is met.

PACE Milestone 3
Complex Sentence Structure (unless)

Context: Rami wants to achieve as many awards as possible in his sports clubs, but he needs to practise and work hard.

Task: Write 3 complex sentences using the subordinating conjunction '**unless**' that relate to the context above.

Practise: Writing a complex sentence using '**unless**' as a subordinating conjunction.
- Leave a line between each sentence.
- Sentences must be punctuated correctly.
- Circle the subject and draw a rectangle around the verb in each clause.

Think about: what Rami need to do if he wants to achieve his awards. Consider what won't happen if he doesn't work hard.

Remember: '**unless**' shows that something will or will not happen '**unless**' another action happens or condition is met.

PACE MILESTONE 3 – COMPLEX SENTENCES (ALTHOUGH, WHILE, UNLESS)

PACE Milestone 3
Complex Sentence Structure ('although', 'while', 'unless')

Context: Your friends and family have gone swimming at the local pool. Some people are excited and organised. Some people are not so confident and have forgotten things they need. Everyone still enjoys themselves and has a fun day.

Task: Write 3 different complex sentences using the subordinating conjunctions '**although**', '**while**', '**unless**' that relate to the context above.

Practise: Writing a complex sentence using '**although**', '**while**', '**unless**' as a subordinating conjunction.

- Leave a line between each sentence.
- Sentences must be punctuated correctly.

Sentence Checklist (Tick off each sentence as you write.) although ☐   while ☐   unless ☐

Challenge: Once you have completed each sentence, circle the subject and draw a rectangle around the verb in each clause.

PACE Milestone 3
Complex Sentence Structure ('although', 'while', 'unless')

Context: Ella's phone is on charge. She tries to think of what she can do while it charges. Mum has lots of suggestions, but they are all related to housework, which Ella hates.

Task: Write 3 different complex sentences using the subordinating conjunctions '**although**', '**while**', '**unless**' that relate to the context above.

Practise: Writing a complex sentence using '**although**', '**while**', '**unless**' as a subordinating conjunction.

- Leave a line between each sentence.
- Sentences must be punctuated correctly.

Sentence Checklist (Tick off each sentence as you write.) although ☐   while ☐   unless ☐

Challenge: Once you have completed each sentence, circle the subject and draw a rectangle around the verb in each clause.

PACE Milestone 3
Complex Sentence Structure ('although', 'while', 'unless')

Context: Bruno is an adventurous puppy and he has managed to get away from his owner. Now Bruno is lost. His owner is looking for him, but Bruno is having too much fun sniffing flowers and chasing other dogs.

Task: Write 3 different complex sentences using the subordinating conjunctions '**although**', '**while**', '**unless**' that relate to the context above.

Practise: Writing a complex sentence using '**although**', '**while**', '**unless**' as a subordinating conjunction.

- Leave a line between each sentence.
- Sentences must be punctuated correctly.

Sentence Checklist (Tick off each sentence as you write.) although ☐   while ☐   unless ☐

Challenge: Once you have completed each sentence, circle the subject and draw a rectangle around the verb in each clause.

PACE MILESTONE 3 – COMPOUND SENTENCES (YET, OR, NOR/FOR) AND COMPLEX SENTENCES (ALTHOUGH, WHILE, UNLESS)

PACE Milestone 3
Compound and Complex Sentence Structures   ('**yet**', '**or**', '**nor**'/'**for**' and '**although**', '**while**', '**unless**')

Context: You are on board a pirate ship. Your captain is Long John Silver and he has a map. You are sailing the seven seas searching for treasure, but there's a storm coming. Other pirate ships are in the area looking for a secret island.

Task: Write 6 different sentences using the coordinating conjunctions '**yet**', '**or**', '**nor**'/'**for**' and the subordinating conjunctions '**although**', '**while**', '**unless**' that relate to the context above. Start with the conjunctions you feel most confident using.

Clauses: Think about varying the position of your main and subordinate clauses in the complex sentences.

Sentence Checklist (Tick off each sentence as you write.)	yet ☐ or ☐ nor/for ☐ although ☐ while ☐ unless ☐

Challenge: Once you have completed each sentence, circle the subject and draw a rectangle around the verb in each clause.

PACE Milestone 3
Compound and Complex Sentence Structures   ('**yet**', '**or**', '**nor**'/'**for**' and '**although**', '**while**', '**unless**')

Context: Think of the story about Goldilocks and the Three Bears. Think about all of the different stages of the story with Goldilocks eating the porridge, sitting in the chairs and sleeping in the beds of the three bears, before they finally come home.

Task: Write 6 different sentences using the coordinating conjunctions '**yet**', '**or**', '**nor**'/'**for**' and the subordinating conjunctions '**although**', '**while**', '**unless**' that relate to the context above. Start with the conjunctions you feel most confident using.

Clauses: Think about varying the position of your main and subordinate clauses in the complex sentences.

Sentence Checklist (Tick off each sentence as you write.)	yet ☐ or ☐ nor/for ☐ although ☐ while ☐ unless ☐

Challenge: Once you have completed each sentence, circle the subject and draw a rectangle around the verb in each clause.

PACE Milestone 3
Compound and Complex Sentence Structures   ('**yet**', '**or**', '**nor**'/'**for**' and '**although**', '**while**', '**unless**')

Context: News has just broken that the internet has broken … forever! Cyber criminals have stolen the code for the internet to work which means there is no social media for children all over the world! Having been forced to find other ways to entertain themselves, millions of children have left their homes and discovered something called 'the Sun'.

Task: Write 6 different sentences using the coordinating conjunctions '**yet**', '**or**', '**nor**'/'**for**' and the subordinating conjunctions '**although**', '**while**', '**unless**' that relate to the context above. Start with the conjunctions you feel most confident using.

Clauses: Think about varying the position of your main and subordinate clauses in the complex sentences.

Sentence Checklist (Tick off each sentence as you write.)	yet ☐ or ☐ nor/for ☐ although ☐ while ☐ unless ☐

Challenge: Once you have completed each sentence, circle the subject and draw a rectangle around the verb in each clause.

PACE MILESTONE 4 – ALL SIMPLE COMPOUND AND COMPLEX SENTENCE TYPES

PACE Milestone 4 covers all simple, compound and complex sentences and provides a clear opportunity for pupils to practise and apply their understanding of each sentence type within different writing contexts. These tasks are more in-depth and cover each sentence type separately, with variation on which conjunctions are required. These are great for regular use within the classroom, due to the substantial nature of the tasks. These PACE tasks provide useful opportunities for teachers to assess pupil competence informally and intervene where necessary with active modelling and sentence-level instruction. This is the '**C**onsolidation and **E**nable' element of PACE.

Once again, the core focus should be around the subject and the main verb, alongside the clause structure and correct punctuation.

PACE Milestone 4
All Simple, Compound and Complex Sentence Structures

Context: It's sports day at school. The sun is shining and there are hundreds of parents on the school field cheering for all the children. There are lots of different races and events. Four of the children taking part are called Ali, Mia, Theo and Mutra. Mr Robson and Mrs Hopson are in charge of all the events. Think about how different pupils might be feeling.

Task One (simple sentence): Write 3 separate, simple sentences that relate to the context above. Circle the subject and draw a rectangle around the verb in each sentence.

Task Two (compound sentence): Write 3 compound sentences that relate to the context above using the coordinating conjunctions '**and**', '**but**', '**so**'. (Tick off each sentence as you write.)

and ☐   but ☐   so ☐

Task Three (complex sentence): Write 3 complex sentences that relate to the context above using the subordinating conjunctions '**because**', '**although**', '**while**'. (Tick off each sentence as you write.)

Tip: Remember to vary your clause structure.

because ☐   although ☐   while ☐

PACE Milestone 4
All Simple, Compound and Complex Sentence Structures

Context: Rudi, Mustafa and Ruby have all been collecting litter in their local area. They want to help the environment, save animals and make their local area a nice place to live. Their friend, Robbie, didn't want to help. He said the litter didn't matter. The trio end up in the local newspaper for their community spirit.

Task One (simple sentence): Write 3 separate, simple sentences that relate to the context above. Circle the subject and draw a rectangle around the verb in each sentence.

Task Two (compound sentence): Write 3 compound sentences that relate to the context above using the coordinating conjunctions '**so**', '**or**', '**but**'. (Tick off each sentence as you write.)

so ☐   or ☐   but ☐

Task Three (complex sentence): Write 3 complex sentences that relate to the context above using the subordinating conjunctions '**unless**', '**if**', '**when**'. (Tick off each sentence as you write.)

Tip: Remember to vary your clause structure.

unless ☐   if ☐   when ☐

Sentence Ninja © Andrew Jennings, 2025

PACE Milestone 4
All Simple, Compound and Complex Sentence Structures

Context: Think about the book you are reading, either as a class or your own personal book. Think about the setting, the characters, and the characters' friends and enemies. How are the characters feeling? What are they thinking? What are they trying to do? What problems do they have?

Task One (simple sentence): Write 3 separate, simple sentences that relate to the context above. Circle the subject and draw a rectangle around the verb in each sentence.

Task Two (compound sentence): Write 3 compound sentences that relate to the context above using the coordinating conjunctions '**nor**', '**and**', '**yet**'. (Tick off each sentence as you write.)

nor ☐   and ☐   yet ☐

Task Three (complex sentence): Write 3 complex sentences that relate to the context above using the subordinating conjunctions '**although**', '**while**', '**because**'. (Tick off each sentence as you write.)
Tip: Remember to vary your clause structure.

although ☐   while ☐   because ☐

PACE Milestone 4
All Simple, Compound and Complex Sentence Structures

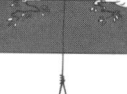

Context: It's the start of the summer holidays. Fran and Alex have discovered an old tree house at the bottom of the farmer's field. It's amazing! It's old but, it has lots of cool features like ladders and ropes. Inside, it has a message from the previous owners, Thomas and Lily. Fran and Alex are so excited about the summer ahead.

Task One (simple sentence): Write 3 separate, simple sentences that relate to the context above. Circle the subject and draw a rectangle around the verb in each sentence.

Task Two (compound sentence): Write 3 compound sentences that relate to the context above using the coordinating conjunctions '**and**', '**so**', '**but**'. (Tick off each sentence as you write.)

and ☐   so ☐   but ☐

Task Three (complex sentence): Write 3 complex sentences that relate to the context above using the subordinating conjunctions '**because**', '**if**', '**unless**'. (Tick off each sentence as you write.)
Tip: Remember to vary your clause structure.

because ☐   if ☐   unless ☐

PACE Milestone 4
All Simple, Compound and Complex Sentence Structures

Context: Vinny visits the pet store with his parents. He is allowed to get a pet for his birthday. There are so many pets to choose from. What is Vinny looking for? What is he allowed? What isn't he allowed? What other items might Vinny and his parents need to buy for his new pet?

Task One (simple sentence): Write 3 separate, simple sentences that relate to the context above. Circle the subject and draw a rectangle around the verb in each sentence.

Task Two (compound sentence): Write 3 compound sentences that relate to the context above using the coordinating conjunctions '**and**', '**but**', '**so**'. (Tick off each sentence as you write.)

and ☐   but ☐   so ☐

Task Three (complex sentence): Write 3 complex sentences that relate to the context above using the subordinating conjunctions '**because**', '**although**', '**while**'. (Tick off each sentence as you write.)
Tip: Remember to vary your clause structure.

because ☐   although ☐   while ☐

PACE Milestone 4

All Simple, Compound and Complex Sentence Structures

Context: Alexia, Ruby and Thea all visit the fairground. Alexia and Ruby love rollercoasters, but Thea doesn't really like rides. There are lots of different rides and activities for the girls to try. Even though some of the queues are really long and the weather isn't great, they all have an amazing time. Thea even discovers that she does actually like certain rides!

Task One (simple sentence): Write 3 separate, simple sentences that relate to the context above. Circle the subject and draw a rectangle around the verb in each sentence.

Task Two (compound sentence): Write 3 compound sentences that relate to the context above using the coordinating conjunctions '**so**', '**or**', '**but**'. (Tick off each sentence as you write.)

so ☐ or ☐ but ☐

Task Three (complex sentence): Write 3 complex sentences that relate to the context above using the subordinating conjunctions '**because**', '**although**', '**while**'. (Tick off each sentence as you write.)

Tip: Remember to vary your clause structure.

because ☐ although ☐ while ☐

PACE Milestone 4

All Simple, Compound and Complex Sentence Structures

Context: The children are learning about the amazing animals that are found in rainforests. Each child has to write about two animals. What animals live in the rainforest? What do they look like? What dangers might they encounter? How and where do they live? What do they eat? Where do they sleep? How do they hunt?

Task One (simple sentence): Write 3 separate, simple sentences that relate to the context above. Circle the subject and draw a rectangle around the verb in each sentence.

Task Two (compound sentence): Write 3 compound sentences that relate to the context above using the coordinating conjunctions '**nor**', '**and**', '**yet**'. (Tick off each sentence as you write.)

nor ☐ and ☐ yet ☐

Task Three (complex sentence): Write 3 complex sentences that relate to the context above using the subordinating conjunctions '**although**', '**while**', '**because**'. (Tick off each sentence as you write.)

Tip: Remember to vary your clause structure.

although ☐ while ☐ because ☐

PACE Milestone 4

All Simple, Compound and Complex Sentence Structures

Context: It's World Book Day. The teachers have arranged lots of fun activities for the children. Three of the children looking forward to the day are Ben, Phil and Rudi. All of the children and teachers are dressed as book characters.

Task One (simple sentence): Write 3 separate, simple sentences that relate to the context above. Circle the subject and draw a rectangle around the verb in each sentence.

Task Two (compound sentence): Write 3 compound sentences that relate to the context above using the coordinating conjunctions '**and**', '**so**', '**but**'. (Tick off each sentence as you write.)

and ☐ so ☐ but ☐

Task Three (complex sentence): Write 3 complex sentences that relate to the context above using the subordinating conjunctions '**because**', '**if**', '**unless**'. (Tick off each sentence as you write.)

Tip: Remember to vary your clause structure.

because ☐ if ☐ unless ☐

PACE MILESTONE 5 – RELATIVE AND EMBEDDED CLAUSES

PACE Milestone 5 includes relative and embedded clause sentences and provides a clear opportunity for pupils to practise and apply their understanding of each sentence type within different writing contexts. These are great for regular use within the classroom, due to the substantial nature of the tasks. These PACE tasks provide useful opportunities for teachers to assess pupil competence informally and intervene where necessary with active modelling and sentence-level instruction. This is the '**C**onsolidation and **E**nable' element of PACE.

Once again, the core focus should be around the subject and the main verb, alongside the clause structure and correct punctuation.

PACE Milestone 5
All Simple, Compound and Complex Sentence Structures (including Relative Clauses)
Context: Lottie is a witch and Max is a wizard. They both live on a mysterious island. Lottie and Max always create spells and potions to cause problems for the local village people. They think it's fun when the villagers get in a bit of bother. The villagers don't like them because of the spells and potions they create and the trouble they cause. Lottie feels bad sometimes but Max doesn't.
Task One (simple sentence): Write 3 separate, simple sentences that relate to the context above. Circle the subject and draw a rectangle around the verb in each sentence.
Task Two (compound sentence): Write 3 compound sentences that relate to the context above using the coordinating conjunctions '**and**', '**but**', '**so**'. (Tick off each sentence as you write.)
and ☐   but ☐   so ☐
Task Three (complex sentence): Write 3 complex sentences that relate to the context above using the subordinating conjunctions '**because**', '**if**', '**unless**'. (Tick off each sentence as you write.)   **Tip:** Remember to vary your clause structure.
because ☐   if ☐   unless ☐
Task Four (relative clause): Write 3 sentences that relate to the context above that contain relative clauses, using the relative pronouns '**who**', '**which**', '**that**'. (Tick off each sentence as you write.)   **Tip:** Vary your clause structure by embedding the relative clause.
who ☐   which ☐   that ☐

PACE Milestone 5
All Simple, Compound and Complex Sentence Structures (including Relative Clauses)
Context: Ria and Paulo are in the library. They are each choosing a new book to read. They both have different tastes; Ria likes adventure and mystery and Paulo likes books that are fun to read. The library is closing soon so they must choose their books quickly.
Task One (simple sentence): Write 3 separate, simple sentences that relate to the context above. Circle the subject and draw a rectangle around the verb in each sentence.
Task Two (compound sentence): Write 3 compound sentences that relate to the context above using the coordinating conjunctions '**but**', '**yet**', '**or**'. (Tick off each sentence as you write.)
but ☐   yet ☐   or ☐
Task Three (complex sentence): Write 3 complex sentences that relate to the context above using the subordinating conjunctions '**although**', '**while**', '**unless**'. (Tick off each sentence as you write.)   **Tip:** Remember to vary your clause structure.
although ☐   while ☐   unless ☐
Task Four (relative clause): Write 3 sentences that relate to the context above that contain relative clauses, using the relative pronouns '**whose**', '**where**', '**when**'. (Tick off each sentence as you write.)   **Tip:** Vary your clause structure by embedding the relative clause.
whose ☐   where ☐   when ☐

PACE Milestone 5
All Simple, Compound and Complex Sentence Structures (including Relative Clauses)

Context: Lucy is going to a concert featuring her favourite musician, Frav Milous. Frav is one of the most famous singers in the world. Lucy is very excited. Lucy's dad is driving her to the concert and he will wait outside until it has finished. Lucy is meeting her friends, Simia and Phoebe. There are thousands of people at the concert and it is noisy and loud. How are the girls feeling? What are they thinking?

Task One (simple sentence): Write 3 separate, simple sentences that relate to the context above. Circle the subject and draw a rectangle around the verb in each sentence.

Task Two (compound sentence): Write 3 compound sentences that relate to the context above using the coordinating conjunctions '**nor/for**', '**so**', '**and**'. (Tick off each sentence as you write.)

nor/for ☐   so ☐   and ☐

Task Three (complex sentence): Write 3 complex sentences that relate to the context above using the subordinating conjunctions '**when**', '**while**', '**although**'. (Tick off each sentence as you write.)

Tip: Remember to vary your clause structure.

when ☐   while ☐   although ☐

Task Four (relative clause): Write 3 sentences that relate to the context above that contain relative clauses, using the relative pronouns '**which**', '**who**', '**where**'. (Tick off each sentence as you write.)

Tip: Vary your clause structure by embedding the relative clause.

which ☐   who ☐   where ☐

PACE Milestone 5
All Simple, Compound and Complex Sentence Structures (including Relative Clauses)

Context: It's lunchtime and Helen is on her way to meet Dilshan and Joel. Everyone is very hungry because it's been a busy morning of learning. Helen, Dilshan and Joel all like different types of foods for different reasons. What are they having for lunch? Why do they like those foods?

Task One (simple sentence): Write 3 separate, simple sentences that relate to the context above. Circle the subject and draw a rectangle around the verb in each sentence.

Task Two (compound sentence): Write 3 compound sentences that relate to the context above using the coordinating conjunctions '**or**', '**yet**', '**so**'. (Tick off each sentence as you write.)

or ☐   yet ☐   so ☐

Task Three (complex sentence): Write 3 complex sentences that relate to the context above using the subordinating conjunctions '**while**', '**because**', '**if**'. (Tick off each sentence as you write.)

Tip: Remember to vary your clause structure.

while ☐   because ☐   if ☐

Task Four (relative clause): Write 3 sentences that relate to the context above that contain relative clauses, using the relative pronouns '**whose**', '**who**', '**when**'. (Tick off each sentence as you write.)

Tip: Vary your clause structure by embedding the relative clause.

whose ☐   who ☐   when ☐

PACE Milestone 5
All Simple, Compound and Complex Sentence Structures (including Relative Clauses)

Context: A family are camping in a field in the Lake District. It's the summer and the sun is warm. The barbecue is being fired up, music is playing and the children are playing games. The dog is sleeping in the sun. It's time to relax and have fun as a family.

Task One (simple sentence): Write 3 separate, simple sentences that relate to the context above. Circle the subject and draw a rectangle around the verb in each sentence.

Task Two (compound sentence): Write 3 compound sentences that relate to the context above using the coordinating conjunctions '**and**', '**so**', '**but**'. (Tick off each sentence as you write.)

and ☐ so ☐ but ☐

Task Three (complex sentence): Write 3 complex sentences that relate to the context above using the subordinating conjunctions '**because**', '**if**', '**unless**'. (Tick off each sentence as you write.)

Tip: Remember to vary your clause structure.

because ☐ if ☐ unless ☐

Task Four (relative clause): Write 3 sentences that relate to the context above that contain relative clauses, using the relative pronouns '**who**', '**which**', '**that**'. (Tick off each sentence as you write.)

Tip: Vary your clause structure by embedding the relative clause.

who ☐ which ☐ that ☐

PACE Milestone 5
All Simple, Compound and Complex Sentence Structures (including Relative Clauses)

Context: An ancient monster called Grendel is attacking the local village. It wants to eat the cows and horses for lunch. The village people call for Beowulf, the local hero who is here to fight and defeat Grendel. What does Grendel look like? What does Beowulf look like? Why is Grendel dangerous? How might Beowulf defeat the beast? What are they both thinking or feeling? What do the villagers want to happen?

Task One (simple sentence): Write 3 separate, simple sentences that relate to the context above. Circle the subject and draw a rectangle around the verb in each sentence.

Task Two (compound sentence): Write 3 compound sentences that relate to the context above using the coordinating conjunctions '**but**', '**yet**', '**or**'. (Tick off each sentence as you write.)

but ☐ yet ☐ or ☐

Task Three (complex sentence): Write 3 complex sentences that relate to the context above using the subordinating conjunctions '**although**', '**while**', '**unless**'. (Tick off each sentence as you write.)

Tip: Remember to vary your clause structure.

although ☐ while ☐ unless ☐

Task Four (relative clause): Write 3 sentences that relate to the context above that contain relative clauses, using the relative pronouns '**whose**', '**where**', '**when**'. (Tick off each sentence as you write.)

Tip: Vary your clause structure by embedding the relative clause.

whose ☐ where ☐ when ☐

PACE Milestone 5
All Simple, Compound and Complex Sentence Structures (including Relative Clauses)

Context: School has decided to serve a super healthy menu for lunch this week to encourage children to try new, healthier food choices. Only fruit, vegetables and pasta are available on the menu. Packed lunches have also been banned. Some children are happy and excited. Some children are really angry about the changes.

Task One (simple sentence): Write 3 separate, simple sentences that relate to the context above. Circle the subject and draw a rectangle around the verb in each sentence.

Task Two (compound sentence): Write 3 compound sentences that relate to the context above using the coordinating conjunctions '**nor/for**', '**so**', '**and**'. (Tick off each sentence as you write.)

nor/for ☐ so ☐ and ☐

Task Three (complex sentence): Write 3 complex sentences that relate to the context above using the subordinating conjunctions '**when**', '**while**', '**although**'. (Tick off each sentence as you write.)

Tip: Remember to vary your clause structure.

when ☐ while ☐ although ☐

Task Four (relative clause): Write 3 sentences that relate to the context above that contain relative clauses, using the relative pronouns '**which**', '**who**', '**where**'. (Tick off each sentence as you write.)

Tip: Vary your clause structure by embedding the relative clause.

which ☐ who ☐ where ☐

PACE Milestone 5
All Simple, Compound and Complex Sentence Structures (including Relative Clauses)

Context: It's Friday morning, the last day of the week. Ali doesn't want to get up for school. He is very tired because he stayed up late reading his book. Mum told him to get to sleep last night and now she's annoyed that he won't get up and get ready for school. If he doesn't hurry up they will be late for school.

Task One (simple sentence): Write 3 separate, simple sentences that relate to the context above. Circle the subject and draw a rectangle around the verb in each sentence.

Task Two (compound sentence): Write 3 compound sentences that relate to the context above using the coordinating conjunctions '**or**', '**yet**', '**so**'. (Tick off each sentence as you write.)

or ☐ yet ☐ so ☐

Task Three (complex sentence): Write 3 complex sentences that relate to the context above using the subordinating conjunctions '**while**', '**because**', '**if**'. (Tick off each sentence as you write.)

Tip: Remember to vary your clause structure.

while ☐ because ☐ if ☐

Task Four (relative clause): Write 3 sentences that relate to the context above that contain relative clauses, using the relative pronouns '**whose**', '**who**', '**when**'. (Tick off each sentence as you write.)

Tip: Vary your clause structure by embedding the relative clause.

whose ☐ who ☐ when ☐

CREATE AND CONNECT

The **Create and Connect** period is all about bringing together everything pupils have learned over the past three years, and dedicating time to creating sentences and connecting ideas together in varied clause structures, with a range of conjunctions and punctuation. This time will allow pupils to develop their ability to be creative with their sentences, while facilitating opportunities to discuss the meaning and impact of the structure of the sentence and its components.

Create and Connect
Simple, Compound, Complex

Context: A brave knight is searching a forbidden forest for an evil witch who has been attacking the local town.

Task: Write 3 sentences that relate to the context above. The first should be a **simple** sentence, the second should be a **compound** sentence and the third should be a **complex** sentence. These sentences should be written one after the other to create a short, three-sentence passage. They can be in any order you choose.

Text Type: Write the sentences in a narrative style, as if you are writing a story.

Sentence Checklist (Tick off each sentence as you write.)	Simple ☐ Compound ☐ Complex ☐

Be ready to share your sentences and explain your sentence structures.

Create and Connect
Simple, Compound, Complex

Context: You need to convince your headteacher that making playtimes at school five minutes longer would be a good thing.

Task: Write 3 sentences that relate to the context above. The first should be a **simple** sentence, the second should be a **compound** sentence and the third should be a **complex** sentence. These sentences should be written one after the other to create a short, three-sentence passage. They can be in any order you choose.

Text Type: Write the sentences in a narrative style, as if you are writing a story.

Sentence Checklist (Tick off each sentence as you write.)	Simple ☐ Compound ☐ Complex ☐

Be ready to share your sentences and explain your sentence structures.

Create and Connect
Simple, Compound, Complex

Context: It's the last minute of a football game and England has been awarded a penalty. Their best player is going to take the kick. Will they score or will they miss?

Task: Write 3 sentences that relate to the context above. The first should be a **simple** sentence, the second should be a **compound** sentence and the third should be a **complex** sentence. These sentences should be written one after the other to create a short, three-sentence passage. They can be in any order you choose.

Text Type: Write the sentences in a narrative style, as if you are writing a story.

Sentence Checklist (Tick off each sentence as you write.)	Simple ☐ Compound ☐ Complex ☐

Be ready to share your sentences and explain your sentence structures.

Create and Connect
Simple, Compound, Complex

Context: Sue is making a jam sandwich. What are the three steps she might take to make the jam sandwich?

Task: Write 3 sentences that relate to the context above. The first should be a **simple** sentence, the second should be a **compound** sentence and the third should be a **complex** sentence. These sentences should be written one after the other to create a short, three-sentence passage. They can be in any order you choose.

Text Type: Write the sentences in a non-fiction style, as if you are writing instructions.

Sentence Checklist (Tick off each sentence as you write.)   Simple ☐   Compound ☐   Complex ☐

Be ready to share your sentences and explain your sentence structures.

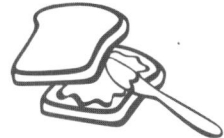

Create and Connect
Simple, Compound, Complex

Context: You are writing a mini-report on animals, focusing on your favourite animal. Provide some information about your favourite animal and its interesting features.

Task: Write 3 sentences that relate to the context above. The first should be a **simple** sentence, the second should be a **compound** sentence and the third should be a **complex** sentence. These sentences should be written one after the other to create a short, three-sentence passage. They can be in any order you choose.

Text Type: Write the sentences in a non-fiction style, as if you are writing a report.

Sentence Checklist (Tick off each sentence as you write.)   Simple ☐   Compound ☐   Complex ☐

Be ready to share your sentences and explain your sentence structures.

Create and Connect
Simple, Compound, Complex

Context: Goldilocks has been caught breaking into the home of the Three Bears! She has caused damage and eaten food from their home.

Task: Write 3 sentences that relate to the context above. The first should be a **simple** sentence, the second should be a **compound** sentence and the third should be a **complex** sentence. These sentences should be written one after the other to create a short, three-sentence passage. They can be in any order you choose.

Text Type: Write the sentences in a narrative style, as if you are writing a story.

Sentence Checklist (Tick off each sentence as you write.)   Simple ☐   Compound ☐   Complex ☐

Be ready to share your sentences and explain your sentence structures.

Create and Connect
Simple, Compound, Complex

Context: Soldiers in World War II are landing on the beaches of Normandy in Higgins Boats. The doors of the boats open and the soldiers flood onto the dangerous beaches.

Task: Write 3 sentences that relate to the context above. The first should be a **simple** sentence, the second should be a **compound** sentence and the third should be a **complex** sentence. These sentences should be written one after the other to create a short, three-sentence passage. They can be in any order you choose.

Text Type: Write the sentences in a non-fiction style, as if you are recounting an event.

Sentence Checklist (Tick off each sentence as you write.)   Simple ☐   Compound ☐   Complex ☐

Be ready to share your sentences and explain your sentence structures.

Create and Connect
Simple, Compound, Complex

Context: Thea steps into a silent and dark room. Lights are flickering. "Hello," she whispers.

Task: Write 3 sentences that relate to the context above. The first should be a **simple** sentence, the second should be a **compound** sentence and the third should be a **complex** sentence. These sentences should be written one after the other to create a short, three-sentence passage. They can be in any order you choose.

Text Type: Write the sentences in a narrative style, as if you are writing a story.

Sentence Checklist (Tick off each sentence as you write.)	Simple ☐ Compound ☐ Complex ☐

Be ready to share your sentences and explain your sentence structures.

Create and Connect
Simple, Compound, Complex

Context: Alexia has a problem. She doesn't know whether to spend her weekend with her best friend or whether to go and visit her auntie. She feels awful either way because she will let someone down.

Task: Write 3 sentences that relate to the context above. The first should be a **simple** sentence, the second should be a **compound** sentence and the third should be a **complex** sentence. These sentences should be written one after the other to create a short, three-sentence passage. They can be in any order you choose.

Text Type: Write the sentences in a narrative style, as if you are writing a story.

Sentence Checklist (Tick off each sentence as you write.)	Simple ☐ Compound ☐ Complex ☐

Be ready to share your sentences and explain your sentence structures.

MAKE THE READER FEEL

Make the reader feel tasks are all about the intent of our sentences. It's no longer just about supporting our pupils to write simple, compound and complex sentences; it's now about the impact those sentences have on the reader and how they make the reader feel or think.

This is another great opportunity for the teacher to model how specific vocabulary within our sentences can help to have an impact on the reader.

Make the Reader Feel
Simple, Compound, Complex

Context: Carl and his family are trapped. A tornado is ripping through their town destroying everything in its path. Carl and his family are hiding in the cellar of their house.

Task: Write 3 sentences that relate to the context above. The first should be a **simple** sentence, the second should be a **compound** sentence and the third should be a **complex** sentence. These sentences should be written one after the other to create a short, three-sentence passage. They can be in any order you choose.

Text Type: Write the sentences in a narrative style, as if you are writing a story.

Sentence Checklist (Tick off each sentence as you write.)	Simple ☐ Compound ☐ Complex ☐
Be ready to share your sentences and explain your sentence structures.	

Make the Reader Feel
Simple, Compound, Complex

Context: Fred had forgotten his homework (again) and Ms Grimwood had already warned him never to forget it again … or else.

Task: Write 3 sentences that relate to the context above. The first should be a **simple** sentence, the second should be a **compound** sentence and the third should be a **complex** sentence. These sentences should be written one after the other to create a short, three-sentence passage. They can be in any order you choose.

Text Type: Write the sentences in a narrative style, as if you are writing a story.

Sentence Checklist (Tick off each sentence as you write.)	Simple ☐ Compound ☐ Complex ☐
Be ready to share your sentences and explain your sentence structures.	

Make the Reader Feel
Simple, Compound, Complex

Context: Jen is wandering across a meadow full of flowers. It's summer and the sun is beaming down on her.

Task: Write 3 sentences that relate to the context above. The first should be a **simple** sentence, the second should be a **compound** sentence and the third should be a **complex** sentence. These sentences should be written one after the other to create a short, three-sentence passage. They can be in any order you choose.

Text Type: Write the sentences in a narrative style, as if you are writing a story.

Sentence Checklist (Tick off each sentence as you write.)	Simple ☐ Compound ☐ Complex ☐
Be ready to share your sentences and explain your sentence structures.	

Make the Reader Feel

Simple, Compound, Complex

Context: Drav and Greg have escaped the king and are riding away from the castle, but they are being chased by the king's guard. Archers on horseback raise their bows as Drav glances back …

Task: Write 3 sentences that relate to the context above. The first should be a **simple** sentence, the second should be a **compound** sentence and the third should be a **complex** sentence. These sentences should be written one after the other to create a short, three-sentence passage. They can be in any order you choose.

Text Type: Write the sentences in a narrative style, as if you are writing a story.

Sentence Checklist (Tick off each sentence as you write.) Simple ☐   Compound ☐   Complex ☐

Be ready to share your sentences and explain your sentence structures.

Make the Reader Feel

Simple, Compound, Complex

Context: Max is the family dog who has become very ill over the last month. Today is going to be Max's last day with the whole family.

Task: Write 3 sentences that relate to the context above. The first should be a **simple** sentence, the second should be a **compound** sentence and the third should be a **complex** sentence. These sentences should be written one after the other to create a short, three-sentence passage. They can be in any order you choose.

Text Type: Write the sentences in a narrative style, as if you are writing a story.

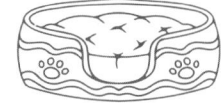

Sentence Checklist (Tick off each sentence as you write.) Simple ☐   Compound ☐   Complex ☐

Be ready to share your sentences and explain your sentence structures.

Make the Reader Feel

Simple, Compound, Complex

Context: Jerry is new at school. It is his first day and already he is starting to make friends.

Task: Write 3 sentences that relate to the context above. The first should be a **simple** sentence, the second should be a **compound** sentence and the third should be a **complex** sentence. These sentences should be written one after the other to create a short, three-sentence passage. They can be in any order you choose.

Text Type: Write the sentences in a narrative style, as if you are writing a story.

Sentence Checklist (Tick off each sentence as you write.) Simple ☐   Compound ☐   Complex ☐

Be ready to share your sentences and explain your sentence structures.

Make the Reader Feel

Simple, Compound, Complex

Context: Alex has been working for months doing odd jobs and being helpful around the village. He wants to buy a new bike for his sister, but he still hasn't saved up enough money.

Task: Write 3 sentences that relate to the context above. The first should be a **simple** sentence, the second should be a **compound** sentence and the third should be a **complex** sentence. These sentences should be written one after the other to create a short, three-sentence passage. They can be in any order you choose.

Text Type: Write the sentences in a narrative style, as if you are writing a story.

Sentence Checklist (Tick off each sentence as you write.) Simple ☐   Compound ☐   Complex ☐

Be ready to share your sentences and explain your sentence structures.

BUILD AND VARY

Build and Vary tasks provide opportunities for pupils to develop high-quality passages of writing that focus on sentence and clause variation, which will support coherence across a paragraph. These activities require pupils to work independently, and will provide them with an opportunity to really demonstrate their core sentence competency. The aim is for pupils to realise that if they can develop varied paragraph size content, ultimately it's just a case of write and repeat to create larger writing outcomes.

Build and Vary	
Simple, Compound, Complex	
Text Type: Adventure – Narrative Fiction	Length: Paragraph

Context: A strange and mysterious fog has covered the land of Grizstrom, Norway. It is a curse from the gods. Max was only a 10-year-old child, but the village elders had tasked him with finding three magical items to lift the curse.

Task: Write a short, creative paragraph based on the context above. There is no limit to the number of sentences you can write. Use a variety of sentence types and clause structures.

Tip: Use the checklist below to tick off sentence types as you structure them, to help you build an awareness of which sentences you have used within the paragraph. There is no need to use every sentence type.

Awareness Checklist: (Tick off each sentence as you write.) simple ☐   however ☐
Compound – coordinating conjunctions: and ☐   but ☐   so ☐   yet ☐   or ☐   nor/for ☐
Complex – subordinating conjunctions: because ☐   if ☐   when ☐   although ☐   while ☐   unless ☐
Relative clause – relative pronoun: who ☐   which ☐   that ☐   whose ☐   where ☐   when ☐

Build and Vary	
Simple, Compound, Complex	
Text Type: Mystery – Narrative Fiction	Length: Paragraph

Context: In the small town of Willow Creek, a famous dinosaur bone has gone missing from the local museum. 13-year-old detective prodigy, Emily, must use her keen observation skills and deductive reasoning to solve the case of the missing dinosaur bone.

Task: Write a short, creative paragraph based on the context above. There is no limit to the number of sentences you can write. Use a variety of sentence types and clause structures.

Tip: Use the checklist below to tick off sentence types as you structure them, to help you build an awareness of which sentences you have used within the paragraph. There is no need to use every sentence type.

Awareness Checklist: (Tick off each sentence as you write.) simple ☐   however ☐
Compound – coordinating conjunctions: and ☐   but ☐   so ☐   yet ☐   or ☐   nor/for ☐
Complex – subordinating conjunctions: because ☐   if ☐   when ☐   although ☐   while ☐   unless ☐
Relative clause – relative pronoun: who ☐   which ☐   that ☐   whose ☐   where ☐   when ☐

Build and Vary

Simple, Compound, Complex

Text Type: Historical – Narrative Fiction	Length: Paragraph

Context: During a family visit to Grandma's house, Sarah goes up into the attic and discovers an old diary belonging to her great-grandmother. As she reads through its pages, she uncovers a hidden family secret that changes everything she thought she knew about her Grandma.

Task: Write a short, creative paragraph based on the context above. There is no limit to the number of sentences you can write. Use a variety of sentence types and clause structures.

Tip: Use the checklist below to tick off sentence types as you structure them, to help you build an awareness of which sentences you have used within the paragraph. There is no need to use every sentence type.

Awareness Checklist: (Tick off each sentence as you write.) simple ☐   however ☐
Compound – coordinating conjunctions: and ☐   but ☐   so ☐   yet ☐   or ☐   nor/for ☐
Complex – subordinating conjunctions: because ☐   if ☐   when ☐   although ☐   while ☐   unless ☐
Relative clause – relative pronoun: who ☐   which ☐   that ☐   whose ☐   where ☐   when ☐

Build and Vary

Simple, Compound, Complex

Text Type: Adventure – Narrative Fiction	Length: Paragraph

Context: On a camping trip in the woods, Sam and his friends stumble upon a mysterious cave entrance. Intrigued by what lies inside they decide to explore, unaware of the ancient treasure and dangers that await them.

Task: Write a short, creative paragraph based on the context above. There is no limit to the number of sentences you can write. Use a variety of sentence types and clause structures.

Tip: Use the checklist below to tick off sentence types as you structure them, to help you build an awareness of which sentences you have used within the paragraph. There is no need to use every sentence type.

Awareness Checklist: (Tick off each sentence as you write.) simple ☐   however ☐
Compound – coordinating conjunctions: and ☐   but ☐   so ☐   yet ☐   or ☐   nor/for ☐
Complex – subordinating conjunctions: because ☐   if ☐   when ☐   although ☐   while ☐   unless ☐
Relative clause – relative pronoun: who ☐   which ☐   that ☐   whose ☐   where ☐   when ☐

Build and Vary

Simple, Compound, Complex

Text Type: Fairy Tale – Narrative Fiction	Length: Paragraph

Context: In a small village by the sea, Lucy befriends a lonely mermaid who longs to explore the world above the waves. Together, they embark on an underwater adventure to find a magical pearl that can grant the mermaid's wish of walking on land.

Task: Write a short, creative paragraph based on the context above. There is no limit to the number of sentences you can write. Use a variety of sentence types and clause structures.

Tip: Use the checklist below to tick off sentence types as you structure them, to help you build an awareness of which sentences you have used within the paragraph. There is no need to use every sentence type.

Awareness Checklist: (Tick off each sentence as you write.) simple ☐   however ☐
Compound – coordinating conjunctions: and ☐   but ☐   so ☐   yet ☐   or ☐   nor/for ☐
Complex – subordinating conjunctions: because ☐   if ☐   when ☐   although ☐   while ☐   unless ☐
Relative clause – relative pronoun: who ☐   which ☐   that ☐   whose ☐   where ☐   when ☐

Build and Vary

Simple, Compound, Complex

Text Type: Mystery – Narrative Fiction | **Length: Paragraph**

Context: During a sleepover at Lily's house, her pet hamster mysteriously disappears from its cage. With her friends by her side, Lily becomes determined to uncover the truth behind the vanishing hamster before the night is over.

Task: Write a short, creative paragraph based on the context above. There is no limit to the number of sentences you can write. Use a variety of sentence types and clause structures.

Tip: Use the checklist below to tick off sentence types as you structure them, to help you build an awareness of which sentences you have used within the paragraph. There is no need to use every sentence type.

Awareness Checklist: (Tick off each sentence as you write.) simple ☐   however ☐
Compound – coordinating conjunctions: and ☐   but ☐   so ☐   yet ☐   or ☐   nor/for ☐
Complex – subordinating conjunctions: because ☐   if ☐   when ☐   although ☐   while ☐   unless ☐
Relative clause – relative pronoun: who ☐   which ☐   that ☐   whose ☐   where ☐   when ☐

Build and Vary

Simple, Compound, Complex

Text Type: Non-Fiction – Instructions | **Length: Paragraph**

Context: Write a set of instructions on how to get ready for school in the morning. Think about some of the everyday, routine things you need to do when you get out of bed.

Task: Write a short, creative paragraph based on the context above. There is no limit to the number of sentences you can write. Use a variety of sentence types and clause structures.

Tip: Use the checklist below to tick off sentence types as you structure them, to help you build an awareness of which sentences you have used within the paragraph. There is no need to use every sentence type.

Awareness Checklist: (Tick off each sentence as you write.) simple ☐   however ☐
Compound – coordinating conjunctions: and ☐   but ☐   so ☐   yet ☐   or ☐   nor/for ☐
Complex – subordinating conjunctions: because ☐   if ☐   when ☐   although ☐   while ☐   unless ☐
Relative clause – relative pronoun: who ☐   which ☐   that ☐   whose ☐   where ☐   when ☐

Build and Vary

Simple, Compound, Complex

Text Type: Narrative – Fiction Sci-Fi | **Length: Paragraph**

Context: You are the captain of a new space rocket that is visiting Mars and you are just about to blast off: 5…4…3…2…1…lift-off! Describe what happens next.

Task: Write a short, creative paragraph based on the context above. There is no limit to the number of sentences you can write. Use a variety of sentence types and clause structures.

Tip: Use the checklist below to tick off sentence types as you structure them, to help you build an awareness of which sentences you have used within the paragraph. There is no need to use every sentence type.

Awareness Checklist: (Tick off each sentence as you write.) simple ☐   however ☐
Compound – coordinating conjunctions: and ☐   but ☐   so ☐   yet ☐   or ☐   nor/for ☐
Complex – subordinating conjunctions: because ☐   if ☐   when ☐   although ☐   while ☐   unless ☐
Relative clause – relative pronoun: who ☐   which ☐   that ☐   whose ☐   where ☐   when ☐

Build and Vary

Simple, Compound, Complex

Text Type: Humour – Narrative Fiction	Length: Paragraph

Context: Today your plate came to life! As you were about to eat your meal, each of the food items on your plate came alive and explained why they shouldn't be eaten and why the other food items on the plate are more delicious. This story is meant to be humorous (funny).

Task: Write a short, creative paragraph based on the context above. There is no limit to the number of sentences you can write. Use a variety of sentence types and clause structures.

Tip: Use the checklist below to tick off sentence types as you structure them, to help you build an awareness of which sentences you have used within the paragraph. There is no need to use every sentence type.

Awareness Checklist: (Tick off each sentence as you write.) simple ☐   however ☐
Compound – coordinating conjunctions: and ☐   but ☐   so ☐   yet ☐   or ☐   nor/for ☐
Complex – subordinating conjunctions: because ☐   if ☐   when ☐   although ☐   while ☐   unless ☐
Relative clause – relative pronoun: who ☐   which ☐   that ☐   whose ☐   where ☐   when ☐

Build and Vary

Simple, Compound, Complex

Text Type: Action/Build-up – Narrative	Length: Paragraph

Context: Today in PE the class is playing rounders. Freddy isn't the most confident catcher so the team put him far out in the deep. The game is close and both sides have a chance of winning. The best hitter comes up to hit. The ball is thrown and Freddy watches from the deep. He wants to be the hero and catch the ball …

Task: Write a short, creative paragraph based on the context above. There is no limit to the number of sentences you can write. Use a variety of sentence types and clause structures.

Tip: Use the checklist below to tick off sentence types as you structure them, to help you build an awareness of which sentences you have used within the paragraph. There is no need to use every sentence type.

Awareness Checklist: (Tick off each sentence as you write.) simple ☐   however ☐
Compound – coordinating conjunctions: and ☐   but ☐   so ☐   yet ☐   or ☐   nor/for ☐
Complex – subordinating conjunctions: because ☐   if ☐   when ☐   although ☐   while ☐   unless ☐
Relative clause – relative pronoun: who ☐   which ☐   that ☐   whose ☐   where ☐   when ☐

Build and Vary

Simple, Compound, Complex

Text Type: Recount – Non-Fiction	Length: Paragraph

Context: Recount your day so far, starting from when you woke up. Include the interesting and not-so-interesting things that have happened up to this point.

Task: Write a short, creative paragraph based on the context above. There is no limit to the number of sentences you can write. Use a variety of sentence types and clause structures.

Tip: Use the checklist below to tick off sentence types as you structure them, to help you build an awareness of which sentences you have used within the paragraph. There is no need to use every sentence type.

Awareness Checklist: (Tick off each sentence as you write.) simple ☐   however ☐
Compound – coordinating conjunctions: and ☐   but ☐   so ☐   yet ☐   or ☐   nor/for ☐
Complex – subordinating conjunctions: because ☐   if ☐   when ☐   although ☐   while ☐   unless ☐
Relative clause – relative pronoun: who ☐   which ☐   that ☐   whose ☐   where ☐   when ☐

Build and Vary
Simple, Compound, Complex

Text Type: Non-Chronological – Non-Fiction	**Length: Paragraph**

Context: Imagine you are an explorer from the past looking for new and undiscovered animals. You come across an animal that no one has ever seen before (we all know the animal now; it could be a tiger or elephant, for example). Describe the animal you have seen for the first time in your explorer's journal.

Task: Write a short, creative paragraph based on the context above. There is no limit to the number of sentences you can write. Use a variety of sentence types and clause structures.

Tip: Use the checklist below to tick off sentence types as you structure them, to help you build an awareness of which sentences you have used within the paragraph. There is no need to use every sentence type.

Awareness Checklist: (Tick off each sentence as you write.) simple ☐   however ☐
Compound – coordinating conjunctions: and ☐   but ☐   so ☐   yet ☐   or ☐   nor/for ☐
Complex – subordinating conjunctions: because ☐   if ☐   when ☐   although ☐   while ☐   unless ☐
Relative clause – relative pronoun: who ☐   which ☐   that ☐   whose ☐   where ☐   when ☐

CHARACTER AND SETTING DESCRIPTION PROMPT

Build and Vary	
Simple, Compound, Complex	
Text Type: Descriptive – Character	Length: Paragraph

Context: Think about a character you have read about in a story. Describe their appearance, personality, the clothes they wear and how they feel.

Task: Write a short, creative paragraph based on the context above. There is no limit to the number of sentences you can write. Use a variety of sentence types and clause structures.

Tip: Use the checklist below to tick off sentence types as you structure them, to help you build an awareness of which sentences you have used within the paragraph. There is no need to use every sentence type.

Awareness Checklist: (Tick off each sentence as you write.) simple ☐ however ☐
Compound – coordinating conjunctions: and ☐ but ☐ so ☐ yet ☐ or ☐ nor/for ☐
Complex – subordinating conjunctions: because ☐ if ☐ when ☐ although ☐ while ☐ unless ☐
Relative clause – relative pronoun: who ☐ which ☐ that ☐ whose ☐ where ☐ when ☐

Build and Vary	
Simple, Compound, Complex	
Text Type: Descriptive – Setting	Length: Paragraph

Context: Think about a setting you have read about in a story. Describe the appearance of the setting and where it is. Include details about the weather, what you can hear or smell and how the setting makes people feel. Use similes or metaphors to help with your description.

Task: Write a short, creative paragraph based on the context above. There is no limit to the number of sentences you can write. Use a variety of sentence types and clause structures.

Tip: Use the checklist below to tick off sentence types as you structure them, to help you build an awareness of which sentences you have used within the paragraph. There is no need to use every sentence type.

Awareness Checklist: (Tick off each sentence as you write.) simple ☐ however ☐
Compound – coordinating conjunctions: and ☐ but ☐ so ☐ yet ☐ or ☐ nor/for ☐
Complex – subordinating conjunctions: because ☐ if ☐ when ☐ although ☐ while ☐ unless ☐
Relative clause – relative pronoun: who ☐ which ☐ that ☐ whose ☐ where ☐ when ☐

ANSWERS

PAGE 28

Subject Strip Circle the subject in each sentence.	**Verb Strip** Draw a rectangle around the verb in each sentence.
The (birds) collected seeds.	Freddy [jumped] on the bed.
My (puppy) chewed the blanket.	Marcus [ate] his yummy pizza.
A (person) was at the door.	[Collect] your rubbish, please.
(We) must visit the library.	I [watched] the film.
(Samiha) drew a picture.	Shall we [rest] on the bench?
The (coffee) was very hot.	I [charged] my phone battery.
Every (meal) was tasty.	Mia [cleaned] her bedroom.
(Dad) rode his bike to work.	The cat [purred] at its owner.
The (children) played on the swings.	The heavy rain [bounced] off the floor.
(Mary) was very happy today.	Mum [poured] Shelly some milk.

PAGE 30

Simple Sentence – Activity 1
Circle the subject and draw a rectangle around the verb.

The (dog) was [sleeping].	(Dani) [tripped] on the rock.
(Mia) [licked] the ice cream.	(Mr Crooks) [read] a book.
A (car) [crashed] into a wall.	The (family) [visited] the park.
(She) [played] on the swings.	(Joseph) [washed] his face.
My (teddy) [fell] onto the floor.	(Shane) [kicked] the ball.
(Sami) [used] his spoon.	(Mum) [paid] for lunch.

Simple Sentence – Activity 2
Circle the subject and draw a rectangle around the verb.

A red (car) [drove] past my house.	(Everyone) [came] for a walk.
The fierce (lion) [roared].	The cold (rain) [hurt] my face.
Yellow (flowers) [danced] in the wind.	(Sam) was [late] for school again.
(I) [heard] the fire alarm.	(We) [collected] litter from our area.
(Jan) [shared] his sweets with me.	Brave (firefighters) [came] to help.
The fluffy (cat) [purred] next to me.	The bright (light) [created] a shadow.

Simple Sentence – Activity 3
Circle the subject and draw a rectangle around the verb.

The old oak (tree) [creaked] in the wind.	(Merlin) [cast] a protection spell.
My (door) [slammed] shut.	(Freddy) [pushed] past Anwar.
The (berries) [tasted] very sweet.	The (sirens) [echoed] for miles.
(Dad) [wanted] to watch the football.	(John) [winked] slyly to his friends.
Our (car) was [covered] in mud.	(Sophie) [studied] modern dance.
The cheeky (squirrel) [stole] the nuts.	Green (flies) [buzzed] all around us.

PAGE 31

Put an S in the box underneath the subject and a V in the box underneath the verb.

The naughty children looked through the dusty window.

☐ S V ☐ ☐ ☐

Put an S in the box underneath the subject and a V in the box underneath the verb.

The beautiful princess escaped from the tower.

☐ ☐ S V ☐ ☐

Put an S in the box underneath the subject and a V in the box underneath the verb.

I slowly climbed the terrifying, rocky mountain.

S V ☐ ☐ ☐

Put an S in the box underneath the subject and a V in the box underneath the verb.

In the distance, a fearsome lion hid in the savannah grass.

☐ ☐ S V ☐

Put an S in the box underneath the subject and a V in the box underneath the verb.

Mr Boddington carefully turned the page of the book.

S ☐ V ☐ ☐

Compound Sentence – Activity 1
Circle each subject and draw a rectangle around each verb in the sentences below.

Clause	Conjunction	Clause
The (girls) [went] to the park,	but	the (boys) [visited] the beach.
(Amy) [kicked] the ball over the fence,	so	(Jenny) [jumped] over to get it.
(Birds) [hunted] for worms,	and	(bees) [buzzed] around the garden.
Should (Mia) [enter] the forest,	or	should (she) [walk] through the swamp?
The (music) [sounded] very loud,	yet	(no one) [minded].
(Andrew) didn't [like] the cold snow,	nor	did (he) [want] to go for a walk in it.
The (lunch box) [was] full,	so	(Paul) [ate] as much as he could.

Compound Sentence – Activity 2
Circle each subject and draw a rectangle around each verb in the sentences below.

Clause	Conjunction	Clause
The (swings) [were] broken,	but	the (children) [had] fun anyway.
(Steph) [tidied] her bedroom,	so	her (friends) could [play].
The (trees) [bent] in the wind,	and	(leaves) [danced] on the ground.
Do (I) [eat] the chocolate bar now,	or	do (I) [save] it for later?
The (alarm) was [ringing] loudly,	yet	(no one) [moved] at all.
(He) didn't [listen] to the advice,	nor	did (he) [revise] for the test.
The (soup) [was] very hot,	so	(Dan) [ate] the sandwich instead.

PAGE 33

Circle each subject and draw a rectangle around each verb in the sentences below.

(Mia) [decided] to play with her friends. (They) [kicked] a football and (they) [played] on the swings. The (girls) [loved] the sun.

Circle each subject and draw a rectangle around each verb in the sentences below.

The (fox) [sneaked] slowly from the bushes and [moved] closer to a picnic. The (picnic) [smelled] so good. The (fox) [licked] her lips, yet (she) [knew] it would be difficult to get the food.

Circle each subject and draw a rectangle around each verb in the sentences below.

It was [snowing] outside, so (Kara) [decided] to build a snowman. The (snow) [fell] harder and harder. The (snow) [covered] Kara's face. The (snowman) [grew] taller, and Kara [added] eyes and a nose.

Circle each subject and draw a rectangle around each verb in the sentences below.

(Daniel) [sat] in the maths lesson, and (he) [listened] carefully to Mrs Francis. The (lesson) [focused] on different triangles. (Daniel) [thought] it was quite easy, yet his (friend) [found] it hard.

Circle each subject and draw a rectangle around each verb in the sentences below.

The (children) [went] to the dinosaur museum on a coach. (Mr Moon) [knew] lots about dinosaurs, so (he) [led] the tour. (Everyone) [learned] a lot of facts, and some (children) [wanted] to come again.

PAGE 63

WORD JUMBLE

The killer whale chased the seal.

My friends are visiting for my birthday.

Mr Robson read the book to the class.

The sun warmed my face.

Alex kicked the ball over the fence.

My sister is walking to the beach.

PAGE 71

CLAUSE COMBINING

Rob put the cutlery on the able, **but** he forgot the table mats.
The sun was warm and relaxing, **yet** the children sat inside watching television.
Alice wanted to play in the garden, **and** she wanted to fill up the paddling pool.
The grass was long and full of weeds, **so** Mum decided to cut the lawn.

Mum was visiting her friend, **and** Dad was painting the shed.
The argument was over, **yet** Marco was still angry.
Jen learned a new dance move, **so** she could impress her friends.
He had enough money to get the bus, **but** he decided to walk anyway.

Arlo sang as loud as he could, **so** his parents could hear him.
The bear devoured the fish, **yet** it was still hungry for more.
He made a huge mistake, **but** he would go on to do it again.
The gravy was very hot, **and** the mashed potato was so soft.

The ants collected the leaves, **so** they could feed the colony.
She stood outside the door, **yet** she was scared to go inside.
Kevin needed to draw a straight line, **but** he didn't have a ruler.
Scarlet brushed her hair, **and** she cleaned her teeth.

PAGE 83
CLAUSE COMBINING

We couldn't play tennis **if** the grass hadn't been cut.
Danny loved reading that book **although** he had read it many times.
There was a small cheer **when** the train arrived into the station.
Freya wasn't coming to the party **because** she had been ill all day.

She was awarded three marks **because** she showed her working out.
Tia played on her phone **while** she had her hair cut.
Tim and Mia had to go to bed **when** the film had finished.
The competition entry wouldn't be accepted **unless** it was handed in on time.

The rabbit chewed the grass **while** the predator watched from the shadows.
There was nothing he could do to win **unless** he was prepared to cheat.
John posted another new video **although** he didn't have many subscribers.
She promised to wash the car **if** she could have five more minutes to read.

The explorer decided to build a shelter **when** the sky started to become dark.
Mia was prepared to be captain **if** no one else was brave enough to do it.
John ordered a vegetable pizza **because** it was his favourite meal.
Petra always followed instructions **unless** she didn't agree with them.